MEL BAY PRESENTS

RYAN'S

Mammoth Collection

1050 REELS and JIGS,

Hornpipes, Clogs, Walk-arounds, Essences, Strathspeys, Highland Flings and Contra Dances, with Figures,

AND HOW TO PLAY THEM.

BY PATRICK SKY

BOWING AND FINGERING MARKED.
TOGETHER WITH

FORTY INTRODUCTORY STUDIES FOR THE VIOLIN, WITH EXPLANATIONS OF BOWING, ETC.

1 2 3 4 5 6 7 8 9 0

CONTENTS

2

4

5

PREFACE

The introduction to this book is abstracted from the original three years of research for my Masters thesis. I was assisted by a number of people to whom I wish to express my profound gratitude: First I want to thank John Hartford, who showed me his copy of *Ryan's Mammoth Collection* and initiated me into fiddle-tune mania. My thanks also to Charles Wolfe, Paul Wells, Kenneth Goldstein, Dan Patterson, and Chris Goertzen. A special thanks to Jill Erikson of the Boston Athenaeum, who turned up Ryan's obituary, to Cathy Sky for editorial advice, to Joe Hickerson of the Library of Congress, and to Loyal Jones of Berea College, for a Mellon Foundation Appalachian Studies Fellowship Grant.

INTRODUCTION

In 1940, the M. M. Cole company published *1000 Fiddle Tunes*. Alan Jabbour's discovery that this book was almost identical to a 19th-century publication entitled *Ryan's Mammoth Collection* quickly aroused the attention of other scholars, notably Charles Wolfe and Paul Wells. When I became interested in the collection in 1985, some scholars and even the catalog staff of the Library of Congress were under the impression that the Ryan of *Ryan's Mammoth Collection* was Sydney Ryan of Boston, author of a series of instrument tutors. But at the Hay Library of Brown University, a copy of Elias Howe's catalog contained an advertisement for *Ryan's Mammoth Collection* which revealed that the author was William Bradbury Ryan.

Although we have considerable documentation of 18th century American music, music of the 19th century, such as *Ryan's Mammoth Collection*, seems to have been ignored, in part because of the sheer volume of material, and in part because 19th-century popular and folk music failed to arouse antiquarian interest. I will attempt to remedy the situation for at least this one music publication so that future musicians and scholars will have a place from which to start a closer examination of Howe and Ryan and their works. Such scholarly interest would not have been accorded them by their contemporaries, one of whom wrote,

> . . . what kind of music is included under the head of copyright? As a general rule the most superficial, trashy stuff that is in vogue: the Negro Melodies (i.e. Minstrel Songs), the namby pamby sentimental ballads, the flashy fantasias, polkas, waltzes, marches, etc. of native American or tenth rate German manufacture thick as leaves on the Vallombrosa. . . .the "Times" and other papers in New York, hail the [music] 'Revolution' with great joy (Dwight 1855:118).

Attitudes toward American popular and traditional music such as those expressed in the above quotation from *Dwight's Journal of Music* prevailed among educated music devotees of the 1850s. As a result, researching popular music from this period, particularly fiddle or dance music, is a frustrating and difficult process. Most 19th-century articles about music dealt with classical music; references to traditional music or popular song were usually disparaging. Nevertheless it was the "minstrel songs, flashy polkas, waltzes, and marches of native American manufacture" that spawned the extremely popular and marketable instrumental anthologies of Elias Howe, and the influential *Ryan's Mammoth Collection.* Ryan's anthology contains evanescent popular and traditional tunes that had, according to their publisher, been taken down by ear from the playing of "Pipers and Violin players, [who] often sang or whistled, they being unable to read music, [so that] the task has been extremely difficult" (Howe 1872:28). By the time that negative attitudes such as those expressed by Dwight receded (with the arrival of music scholars and enthusiasts such as Francis O'Neill, Samuel Bayard, and Ira Ford in the 20th century), it was too late to document fully the music of the era in question. However, Howe's works and *Ryan's Mammoth Collection* contain a substantial portion of the surviving written records of these times.

American Music Publishing in the 19th Century

To understand the tune books of Elias Howe and William Bradbury Ryan one must see them in the context of the history of American music publishing. This activity began in earnest late in the 18th century. Before, and for decades after the American Revolution, most professional musicians in the United States were immigrants from England. Most songs popular here came out of the British broadside operas, while much of the market for instrumental airs was satisfied by the tunebooks of John Playford (1623-1686), imported from England (Lamb 1980:97). Playford's many books included *An Introduction To The Skill Of Music* (1654), eleven editions of which were printed by 1687, and *The English Dancing Master* (1651), with eighteen editions printed through 1728. This was the first instrumental tune book of any consequence in the English-speaking world. All of Playford's books were widely distributed throughout the British Empire, including the American colonies.

After the Revolution, American printing of music increased, especially in sheet-music form. In order to sell sheet music one must have a market of people that are musically literate and sufficiently affluent. At first the numbers of such potential buyers must have been quite small, but this was to change rapidly. American publishers, also limited in number, consisted of individuals who composed, published, and promoted their own music—such as Benjamin Carr of New York and Philadelphia, and his father Joseph Carr of Baltimore (Smith 1980:822).

The Carrs were a father-and-son team who came to America after achieving popularity in England. They brought their success with them, becoming the darlings of the American stage and the founding fathers of American music publishing. Benjamin Carr's song "Hail Columbia, Happy Land" was a Revolutionary War favorite (Chase 1987:117).

Religiously oriented composers and teachers played an important role in encouraging music literacy. Musician, song writer, and teacher William Billings published his *The Singing Master's Assistant* (1778) and *The New England Psalm Singer* (1779). These books, written for unaccompanied four-part voices, included both sacred and secular selections. Billings presented them as models for teaching readers how to read music notation (McKay 1980:703). Publications following Billings' example included: Daniel Reed's *American Singing Book* (1785) and Jacob French's *The New American Melody* (1789). These and other tune books designed as tutors began to appear at an accelerated rate toward the end of the 18th century. Around 1800 a clarinet player named Samuel Holyoke published *The Instrumental Assistant*, the first American collection of tunes for band instruments. In 1811, Edward Riley, an Englishman residing in New York, published the first volume of his famous *Riley's Flute Melodies*, containing 356 tunes. In 1820, Vol. 2 was released; it contains 353 tunes. Before Howe's activity these may have been the largest and most widely distributed tune books in the United States. Not long afterward, in 1837, the Boston school district introduced music instruction into their curriculum. Private schools, such as the Boston Academy, graduated large numbers of musically literate students and became models for other music schools that spread throughout the country.

Beginning in 1820, the Chickering piano company, with its relatively inexpensive mass-produced instruments, helped establish sheet music as a fixture in affluent homes (Rippin 1980:702). Within 20 years the number of music readers in the United States was significant and widespread. The ability to read music had become a status symbol. New compositions were eagerly purchased, and the blossoming American publishing industry rushed to fill orders.

Much has been recently written about music publishing in the 19th century (see Harry Dichter and Elliott Shapiro's *The Handbook of Early American Sheet Music 1768-1889* [1941] and Richard Wolfe's *Secular Music In America 1801-1825* [1964], but very little was written by the publishers themselves. Publishers such as the Oliver Ditson Company were very secretive, regarding their business affairs as confidential and refusing to publicize their activities. They printed little information on their song sheets other than price, title, and author. Even after copyright laws came into being,[1] only rarely did such companies print the copyright dates. However, the formation of the "Board of Music Trade," an association of music publishers, in the 1850s was a major step toward documenting music publishing in America. In 1870 the Board issued its first *Complete Catalogue of Sheet Music and Musical Works*, a list of 80,000 pieces of sheet music, publications and publishers, drawing on the holdings of the Board's twenty member companies. Although this publication listed some of the authors, it omitted copyright dates (Epstein 1973:5). Despite its limitations, the information contained in the catalog is invaluable when it is cross-referenced with other documents of the time. It provides important clues to researchers attempting to date 19th-century songs and tunes.

To the music publishers of the 19th century, ownership of a piece of music was an imprecise concept. They often reissued tunes and songs in various formats without remunerating the composer. Even a successful musician and writer such as Stephen Foster, whose compositions sold millions of copies, could die in poverty—a result, in part, of weak copyright protection and the dishonesty of publishers.

A frequent publisher's tactic was to claim that one of its staff writers composed a piece that actually already existed. *The New York Herald* in October 1869 commented on the music trade as follows:

> Music publishing in this country requires a great deal of improvement. First there is a monopoly called the Board of Music Trade. . . This board meets every summer and now it only amounts to a monopoly for the purpose of grinding down poor American composers to the very dust (Epstein 1970:x-xi).

The Board of Trade was formed in about 1855 (Epstein 1973:vii) in order to dominate a lucrative market; its catalog furthered these intentions. *The New York Times* commented on Jan. 5, 1855:

> The great revolution in the music trade . . . is destined to have a very important bearing on the musical taste in America. We have often wondered that so high prices should be charged for music where nothing was paid for the copyright and the expense was only for engraving, printing and paper (Epstein 1973:vii).

But non-member publishers such as Elias Howe continued to subvert the intended monopoly by publishing works for reasonable prices, perhaps a contributing factor in the eventual disbanding of the Board of Trade around 1895. In any case the careers of the chief publishers of vernacular instrumental tune collections continued publishing beyond the control of official institutions such as the Board of Music Trade.

Elias Howe and
William Bradbury Ryan

Around 1883, Elias Howe of Boston, Massachusetts, published *William Bradbury Ryan's MAMMOTH COLLECTION of more than 1050 Reels and Jigs, Hornpipes, Clogs, Walk Arounds, Slip Jigs, Essences, Strathspeys, Highland Flings and Contra Dances with Figures*. Neither Howe nor the compiler, Ryan, could have known that this tune book would be in circulation for over fifty years as *Ryans's Mammoth Collection*, and then be released again in 1940 (stripped of all references to either Ryan or Howe) by the M. M. Cole Company, and published as *One Thousand Fiddle Tunes. Ryan's Mammoth Collection*, then, has been in publication for over 100 years, and has sold many thousands of copies.

This book is one of the richest and most interesting of the 19th-century instrumental collections, and is a bonanza for students of American vernacular music. Examining the music that it contains will help us understand how the cross-cultural exchange between minstrel shows, ethnic musics, and even classical music influenced some of the genres of what we now call American music.

Although the book was the child of William B. Ryan, the underlying force and surely the major source of inspiration for it was Elias Howe. A study of the book properly needs to begin with him.

Elias' family was descended from John Howe, an early settler of Sudbury, Massachusetts (New England Historical and Genealogical Society 1895:480). The Howes, like the Lowells, are one of the old New England families that have produced an inordinate number of talented people. Among the well-known Howes were another Elias Howe, who invented the sewing machine; Julia Ward Howe, author, poet, and legendary composer of "The Battle Hymn of the Republic"; and our Elias Howe, fiddle player and publisher.

Elias Howe was born to Elias and Hannah (Perry) Howe of Framingham, Massachusetts, in 1820. He was the last of five children. Howe's parents were of modest means, and Elias, like most children of that time, had to find employment at an early age. He obtained a job with a neighbor as a plowboy with a salary of two cents per day. During this time, he obtained a violin tutor and learned to play the fiddle. He listened to the local fiddlers and copied their tunes down into a blank book. His music commonplace book became very popular; local musicians and friends constantly borrowed it to use as a source book for tunes to play at the local dances. Young Howe must have realized the market potential of a large collection of tunes and organized his manuscript into a book for publication. At the age of twenty, Howe offered his collection to the Boston firm of Kidder and Wright. He was told that it would cost him 500 dollars to publish the book. Howe did not have the money, but told the publishers that he would "work his legs off to make the book successful" (Herndon 1892:266). He must have given a convincing argument because the firm published the book in 1840 under the title *The Musician's Companion*. The bargain struck was that, if Kidder and Wright would put up the publishing money, then Howe would purchase the books from them as fast as he could sell them. Howe borrowed money and made his first purchase, but quickly suffered a major setback when the leading music stores refused to handle the book, fearing that marketing the book would undercut their sales of single sheet music items (Herndon 1892:266).

During the middle 1800s, music was sold in sheet music form and was very expensive, going for as much as twenty five cents per item. Major publishers such as the Oliver Ditson Company had a near-monopoly on the music publishing industry in the United States. These large companies not only published and distributed most of the music in America, but in addition owned a majority of the retail music stores; they also manufactured musical instruments. Undeterred,

Howe set out selling his book door to door, through street vendors and at news stands (Herndon 1892:266).

The Musician's Companion (1840) and subsequent books of Howe's that followed, were printed on cheap newsprint and bound with cardboard. They contained hundreds of tunes and were among the first music books at a "popular price" published in the United States, selling for a then remarkably low price of around fifty cents. *The Musician's Companion* was an instant success; within two years Howe sold enough books to buy the plates back and to go into business for himself. In 1842 he opened his first store, in Providence, Rhode Island. In this store, at 98 Westminster Street, he sold sheet music and repaired both musical instruments and umbrellas. Eventually he expanded *The Musician's Companion* to three volumes, and sold many thousands of copies. In 1843 Howe moved from Providence to Boston, where he opened a store at 7 Cornhill Street (now renamed Washington Street). He continued collecting tunes from musicians. By adding these tunes to ones that he borrowed from other tune books, he cut and pasted large numbers of books. "In a statement made in 1888 Howe claimed the number of his publications to be around 200" (New England Genealogical Society 1895:480).

Elias Howe

A measure of Howe's success was the fact that in 1845 he moved to 56 Court Street in Boston, and became a partner of Henry Tolman of the firm of Russell and Tolman, a large and successful publishing house. This new firm then published *Howe's Accordeon Instructor* (1845), which soon sold one hundred thousand copies[2] (Temple 1887:601). The partnership with Tolman was short-lived; in 1850 Howe sold most of his catalog to the Oliver Ditson Company. The transaction made him enough money to buy the estate of Seth B. Howes in Framingham, Massachusetts (Herndon 1892:265). The agreement with Ditson was that Howe was to remain out of the publishing business for a period of ten years and that he would sign over all of the publications that he owned. Among the works transferred to Ditson were *Howe's Accordion Without a Master* (1851), *Howe's School for Violin* (1860), and *Howe's School for the Flageolet* (1858). Later additions by Howe to the Ditson catalog included works that appeared under pseudonyms: a collection of the songs of the Christy Minstrels, issued under the amusing pen name of "Gumbo Chaff"; *Songs of Ireland*, (ca.1882) under the name of Patrick O'Flannigan; and one under the name of "Mary O'Neill" (N.E. Genealogical and Historical Society. 1895:480). Exactly how many works Howe had completed by this time, or how many were transferred to Ditson, is unknown. According to Roorbach's *Catalogue of American Publications*, of the seventeen works published by Howe, only nine went to Ditson (Roorbach 1852:270).[3] Early accounts of Howe's life state that Howe sold his entire catalog to Ditson (Ayers 1937:12-15), but this does not appear to be true.

Since the agreement was that Howe was to refrain from publishing for ten years, it appears that Howe intended to change careers. He obtained a regular job as the manager of an ice company in South Reading. However, in his spare time he continued to assemble instructional tune books, some of which he published with Balmer and Webber of New York and with the Switt Company of Louisville, Kentucky (Roorbach 1852:141-142).

When Howe returned to full-time publishing in 1860, he became the most prominent instructional tune book publisher in the United States. During the period between 1860 and 1870, Howe produced some of his most ambitious works. Two of these were monumental even by 20th-century standards. The first of these was *Howe's One Thousand Jigs and Reels* (ca. 1867), (the title actually reads *Howe's One Thousand Jigs and Reels: Clog Dances, Contra Dances, Fancy Dances, Hornpipes, Strathspeys, Breakdowns, Irish Dances, Scotch Dances, &c., &c., for the Violin, Flute, Clarionet, Cornet, Fife, Flageolet, or any treble instrument*); the other work was the *Musician's Omnibus*, ca.1864, the largest collection of tunes that has ever been published in the United States. Howe continued with this series. Each volume contained around 600 tunes. The *Musician's Omnibus* reached seven volumes by 1882, and contained a staggering total of 6500 pieces ranging from operatic arias to Irish jigs. The entire collection was called *The Quintuple Musician's Omnibus*. All volumes were arranged for treble instruments such as violin, flute, clarinet, cornet, fife, and flageolet.

In 1861, the War Between the States opened up a new avenue for the enterprising Howe: manufacturing drums for the Massachusetts Regiments of the Union Army. He also sold fifes manufactured by the grandson of Jacob Astor. President Lincoln sent for Howe and offered him the Army position of Director of Bands at the rank of Lt. Colonel, an offer which Howe declined. Perhaps Howe reasoned that he could be of better use supplying drums, fifes, and most importantly, fife instructional tune books, or perhaps he simply wished to avoid an interruption in his income. Howe made a great deal of his money with these fife tutors. Ironically, Howe discovered after the war that the majority of the books were distributed to the Rebel armies, probably by way of Louis Tripp of the Tripp and Cragg Co. of Louisville, Kentucky (Ayars 1937:12-15).

Howe was touched by the war in another way. During or before 1865 William Bradbury Ryan came to work for Howe's company, then located at 103 Court Street, Boston. Ryan had been born in Lyndon, Vermont, in 1831, and attended Old Saint Johnsbury Academy. Arriving in Boston in 1850, he first worked for an uncle as a grocer (Boston Globe 1910:8). He was first listed in the Boston Directory in 1854 as living at a boarding house on 55 Lowell Street. His occupation is then listed as porter (Adams 1854:267). In 1861 Ryan is listed in the Directory as living at 24 1/2 Winter Street. He is called a musician, but unfortunately the directory does not tell what instrument Ryan played. Also, a quick look at the Directory's band listings for that year reveals that Ryan did not have his own band at this time. During the spring of 1861 Ryan joined Colonel Slocum's 2nd Rhode Island Regiment as a musician in the band under the command of his longtime friend, bandleader Peter Kalkarnin (Woodbury 1875:19). During this same period Howe was located nearby at 33 Court Street. Whether or not Ryan was working for Howe at this time is not clear.

In June of 1861, Ryan's regiment was sent to Camp Sprague, just outside of Washington, D.C., where it remained camped for a month. It moved to Virginia in July, just in time to get caught up in the first battle of "Manassas" or "Bull Run." The 2nd Rhode Island regiment was completely destroyed, leaving only 80 survivors; Colonel Slocum was among those killed. During the ensuing rout of the Union armies, Ryan was captured by the Confederates while aiding the injured. Ryan could have escaped at the time, but chose to continue helping the wounded of both sides. Assigned to the Cavalry of J.E.B. Stuart as a prisoner, Ryan was moved to Sudley Church, where a hospital had been set up. There he continued to aid the wounded. While working there Ryan helped two Union soldiers escape. Ryan, along with several other prisoners, was sent to Richmond, where he was incarcerated for an additional four months. In all he spent about one year as a prisoner of the rebels (**Globe** 1910:8 and **Transcript** 1910:4). He was paroled and released in Washington, North Carolina, on October 15, 1862, and discharged in Boston that same year (Dyer 893:195). According to his obituary, Ryan entered Howe's employment after returning to Boston; the obituary also states that Ryan worked for Howe for thirty years (Globe 1910:8). Since Howe died in 1895, this would place the date of Ryan's initial employment with Howe at 1865.

It appears that Howe's store was at the center of a large network of bands. Although **The Handbook of Early American Sheet Music** (Dichter 1977:208) does not list Howe's address for 1865, we know from the cover of several of Howe's publications that by 1864 he was operating out of 103 Court Street. In the 1860s **The Boston Directory** gives his Court Street address for a growing number of other musicians and bands (Adams 1864:437). In 1861, the Boston Brass Band had been the only band listed in the directory at this address (Adams 1861:523). By 1865, as the war was drawing to a close, there were seven bands listed at 103 Court Street, including Christie's Quadrille Band, Edmond's Quadrille Band, Gilmore's Band [P.S. Gilmore], Humphrie's Band, The Metropolitan Brass Band, Rowell's Quadrille Band, and Ryan's Band [W.B. Ryan] (Adams 1865:497). According to the **Boston Directory**, the number of bands at Howe's address peaked at fifteen in 1870, though all were gone by 1876. Other bands operated from Washington Street, which was adjacent to Court Street. Perhaps Howe was a booking agent or perhaps bands were just operating out of his store. That Howe and Ryan were associated with these bands is implied by the fact that the names of some of these band leaders, such as Jimmy Norton (the "Boss Jig player"), James Hand, and P.S. Gilmore, were later to appear in tune titles in **Ryan's Mammoth Collection**.

Second Rhode Island Regimental Band   *Reproduced from the Collections of the Library of Congress*

From 1861 to 1876 there were two general types of bands—the brass band and the quadrille or dance band. Both Ryan and Howe showed a keen interest in dance bands. In *Howe's Complete Catalogue* (ca. 1882) we find a number of publications specifically written for dance bands. Notice the instrumentation: *Howe's Full Quadrille Orchestra, for Violins, Clarionet, Coronet, Bass, Flute, Viola, Trombone, Cello and Piano,* and *The Quintette Quadrille Band, for Violin, Coronet, Clarionet and Bass.*

By 1870, Howe had relocated to 88 Court Street with his new assistant Ryan, and was once again publishing books; among these was Howe's *Eclectic* series, books of Irish and Scots songs, sentimental songs, and duets for various instruments. His store was now supplying musicians with strings and other paraphernalia, and offering repairs on instruments, in particular violins.

The 1870 Board of Music Trade's *The Complete Catalogue of Sheet Music and Musical Works* credits 43 works to Howe. These works were distributed by three major publishers: 23 by the Oliver Ditson Company, Boston; 11 by S. T. Gordon of New York; and 17 by Balmer and Webber of St. Louis. The catalog also lists *The Musician's Companion*, originally published by S. Phillips and Co., as now being published by Ditson.

Some of Howe's musical activities were non-profit. In 1871 he started collecting rare old stringed instruments, concentrating on violins, banjos, guitars, and less common instruments such as the viola da gamba. He travelled around the world to expand his collection. Once again his hobby met with success: his collection became the largest in the United States.

In 1882, William Bradbury Ryan and his mentor Elias Howe published *William Bradbury Ryan's Mammoth Collection* (copyright 1883),[4] later issued simply as *Ryan's Mammoth Collection*. This single volume is one of the most important repositories of 19th-century American music created for or by blackface minstrel shows, songwriters, instrumental musicians, singers, and dancers, trained or traditional—the music that eventually developed into such 20th-century forms as blues, country music, ragtime, etc.

This enormously popular work contains 1050 tunes for the fiddle, or, as Howe said in his advertisements "any treble instrument." It also contains dance instructions for then popular (but now archaic) dances such as gallops, lancers, and walk-arounds; it includes works by composers such as James Hand, Jimmy Norton, and the famous composer of "Dixie," Dan Emmett. Tunes were titled in honor of generals, dancers, and even royalty (as in the case of "The Prince Charles' Jig"). There are sections dedicated to traditional melodies respectively of England, Scotland, Ireland, Germany, and America.

Ryan and Howe also deserve credit as the most important collectors of Irish dance music in America before Francis O'Neill, the Chief of the Chicago Police Department at the beginning of the 20th century. O'Neill penned several books about Irish music. His *O'Neills Dance Music of Ireland* (1907), containing 1800 tunes, is the largest modern collection of Irish instrumental dance music. The three principal collectors of Irish music during the late 18th and the 19th centuries were Edward Bunting, George Petrie and P.W. Joyce; but their collections were never widely disseminated in the United States (Bunting 1796, Petrie 1855, and Joyce 1873).

In the introduction to his book *Waifs and Strays of Gaelic Melody* (1922), O'Neill remarked that, "Of the 2819 numbers in the Bunting, Petrie and Joyce collections combined, 300 or about eleven percent would be a liberal estimate of the tunes which may be regarded as Jigs, Reels, Hornpipes or Longdances"(p. 5).

The approximately 600 Irish dance tunes collected by Howe and Ryan far exceeds the combined number of dance tunes collected by Bunting, Petrie and Joyce. It would be 40 years after the publication of *Ryan's Mammoth Collection* before O'Neill would publish his massive work. Oddly enough, O'Neill never mentions Ryan, though he seems to have taken a number of tunes from *Ryan's Mammoth Collection*. These include the "Cameronian Reel" (p. 731 in *O'Neills Dance Music of Ireland* and p. 6 in *Ryan's Mammoth Collection*), and "Miss Johnsons" (p. 626 in *O'Neills Dance Music of Ireland* and p. 8 in *Ryan's Mammoth Colletion*).

14

Despite the fact that O'Neill collected a significant number of his tunes from live musicians, he, like Howe and others before him apparently added to his own publications through the time-honored practice of cutting and pasting from previous collections. However, O'Neill did mention Howe in passing when discussing "Turkey in the Straw" (#254 in **Waifs and Strays of Gaelic Melody**). Thus, O'Neill knew of Howe and probably of Ryan, and drew on their collections for tunes. Since O'Neill's time, most scholars of Irish music (e.g., Breandan Breathnach, author of **Folkmusic and Dances of Ireland**) have ignored Howe and Ryan when discussing the great collectors of Irish music.

Elias Howe died in 1895, leaving his business to his sons William Hills Howe and Edward Frank Howe. In 1898 the business was incorporated by them as the Elias Howe Company, which gradually stopped publishing and ceased entirely by 1910. However, the company continued as a music store and instrument repair shop through 1931, when the business was sold. The music plates, by that time too old to be of use, were destroyed (Ayers 1937:15).

After Howe's death, William Bradbury Ryan published on his own for five years. He was listed in the Boston directories as publisher at 88 Court Street, Room #5 (Adams 1896:1335). During this period he published two collections: **Wayside Gleanings** (ca.1895), a collection of fiddle tunes, and **The Busy Bee** (ca.1895), a collection in two volumes.[5] In addition, he also published at least twenty original compositions, including polkas, gallops, etc. Around 1900 Ryan retired. He lived quietly until his death in December of 1910.

In the 1890s, and sporadically through the early 1900s, **Ryans Mammoth Collection** was listed in the **Sears Catalog**. An advertisement in the 1897 edition describes **Ryan's Mammoth Collection** as "A very popular collection of lively music arranged for the violin" (Wolfe 1987:6). The **Sears Catalog** was distributed to millions of American homes; no item got space in it unless the sales figures were significant. The impact of the **Sears Catalog** (not to forget the **Montgomery Ward Catalog**) on American music cannot be measured. These early catalogs contained page after page of musical instruments: banjos, guitars, and others too numerous to list. It was the **Sears Catalog** that first brought large numbers of manufactured musical instruments into the homes of isolated American communities and families. Along with instruments, Sears sold music for zither, violin, harp, and dulcimer and many assorted instruction books including **Ryan's Mammoth Collection**. Also in the same catalogs could be found **Howe's Violin Without a Master** (Sears 1906:256), and **The Musician's Omnibus Complete**, containing 1500 tunes for $.68 (Sears 1906:347).

In summary, Kenneth Goldstein has pointed out that the 1860s was a musically creative and turbulent period. Songsters "sold by the truck loads." The Hutchison Family were at the peak of their popularity (personal conversation 1992). The minstrel show had reached its popular zenith, and road shows of every description were traveling all over the United States. In short, a music boom took place in the middle of the 19th century that included not only song and dance but also instrumental music and especially music for the violin and for the banjo, and Howe and his associates were participants in it. Both Howe and Ryan had long and successful careers spanning over half of the 19th century. They were involved in all aspects of American music, not only as musicians and composers, but as the most successful American tune book publishers of their time. Gaining admittance to the **Sears Roebuck** catalog reflected not only the significance of their accomplishments, but was an accurate measure of their achievements.

From *Ryan's Mammoth Collection* to *1000 Fiddle Tunes*

The original **Ryan's Mammoth Collection**, reproduced here in fascimile, is a tune book that measures roughly eight by eleven inches. It had a red cover and was printed in both soft cover and hardcover. There are 1050 tunes, including a four-page violin tutor in the back of the book containing 40 "studies." It prints four or five tunes to the page; the tunes are not numbered. The book totals 270 pages and an index listing the tunes by page number only. The printing plates were hand engraved. It is the inconsistency of the hand engraving that proves that *1000 Fiddle Tunes* is the same book.

The most influential of Howe's publications, **Howe's 1000 Jigs and Reels**, would seem to be the forerunner of **Ryan's Mammoth Collection** (1883). The size, format, and especially layout and design of the two tunebooks are almost identical. However, **Howe's One Thousand Jigs and Reels** contained very few pieces that Howe had not previously anthologized. By the late 1860s he had an enormous number of tunes in stock. In addition to cutting and pasting to make new books out of old, Howe also used another technique to increase his publications; simply substituting the name of one instrument for another, leaving the tunes the same. For example, by editing and rearranging the layout, he might turn a violin Instructor into a flute or fife Instructor. Goertzen tallied and named 39 tunes that Howe most often included in his tune books, for example "The Devil's Dream," "Rickett's Hornpipe," and "Durang's Hornpipe" (Goertzen 1983:110). These melodies naturally found their way into *Ryan's Mammoth Collection*. One of *Howe's 1000 Jigs and Reels'* claims to fame lies in the fact that it was perhaps "the first book to use the term 'Breakdown' to describe a fiddle tune" (Wolfe 1987:5).

Howe's 1000 Jigs and Reels contained 1000 tunes, as did both volumes 6 and 7 of **The Musician's Omnibus**. Howe obviously realized the market potential and psychological value of the eye-catching number 1000.

What were the tune books from which Howe borrowed? In my copy of **Howe's Musician's Omnibus No. 7** (1882) the heading on page 610 reads: "**Contra Dances—from a collection published about 1703.**" An anonymous annotator marked, in page margins of my copy, 135 tunes and titles spanning pages 610-621 as "exact" or "identical" to those found in Playford's **English Dancing Master** (1716), a collection which appeared in many editions following its first publication in 1651. More recent sources that Howe drew on included publications such as **Riley's Flute Melodies** (1814). This tune book, first published in New York, contains such old and popular tunes as "Haste to the Wedding" and "Flowers of Edinburgh," two tunes that are in current fiddlers' repertories. Another tune listed by Riley as "Shillinaguira"[6] (p. 14) is a jig that can be found in many of Howe's books, and is also listed in *Ryan's Mammoth Collection* as the "Shee La Na Quira Jig" (p. 122). Ryan's version is almost identical to the form in *Riley's Flute Melodies*. We must remember that before the protection of copyright law it was common practice among many or most publishers to take and use whatever was available. This practice of publishing material from any available source contributed greatly to Howe's success.

1,000 Fiddle Tunes is known to many of today's musicians as the "Fiddlers' Bible." It measures nine by twelve inches and contains 1000 tunes but no fiddle tutor. There are eight tunes to the page and the index contains only page numbers, the same as in *Ryan's Mammoth Collection*. It appears that the same plates were used in the printing process of *1,000 Fiddle Tunes*; however, the plates are smaller in size by 20 percent. I do not know how this reduction in size was accomplished. In its index, tunes are classified in just five genres of "fiddle" tunes: reels, jigs, hornpipes, clogs, and strathspeys. *Ryan's Mammoth Collection* listed nine types: reels, jigs, hornpipes, clogs, walk arounds, essences, flings, strathspeys, and contradances, with figures [instructions]. However, Ryan's emphasis is on "dance" figures, some of which would mean nothing to Cole's audience.

In *1000 Fiddle Tunes* a "reel" is simply a type of fiddle tune in 4/4 time; there are no dance figures. In America very few 19th century dances have survived in rural tradition (except for clogging and contradancing) while many of the tunes have remained popular. Most tunes today are usually taken out of the context of the dance and played for aesthetic enjoyment. In the 19th century this was more rarely the case; during this period publishers such as Howe and O'Neill used the term *dance* in the titles of their collections. To my knowledge they never employed the term *fiddle tune.*

In America, Great Britain, and Ireland, the staple dances for almost 200 years were the reel, the jig, and the hornpipe. As early as the 1700s, dancing masters were on the road teaching the latest dances in every village for a fee. Every large city in America, in time, would sport its dance halls. New dances were created at an astonishing rate, and performed by popular dance bands. Many now rare or defunct dances such as quadrilles, mazurkas, the barn dance, redowas, polkas and marches could be found for a generation or more throughout the U.S.A. In the earliest publications of Elias Howe, most of these then-young dances were represented. However, by the 1870s, many of the dances had fallen from popularity; *Ryan's Mammoth Collection*, for example, lists no quadrilles, breakdowns, mazurkas, quicksteps, or polkas. Although a number of these dances survive in other countries, in America the reel, now called a breakdown or hoedown, and the waltz have come to dominate folk dancing, while other genres survive only as fiddle tunes. The majority of melodies once popular as hornpipes and polkas are now played in America as reels.

Many genres in triple or compound time (such as the jig) have all but disappeared in most parts of the U.S., with the exception of New England. This is due, in my opinion, at least in part to the popularity and influence of the five-string banjo. The banjo, played in the style of early blackface minstrelsy and retained in rural tradition as clawhammer style, accommodates duple meters only. This is evidenced by a number of tunes in *Ryan's Mammoth Collection* that are called *jigs.* Instead of being in triple or compound meter, they are in duple time and are idiomatic for the banjo. Indeed, many of them were composed by famous banjo players such as Dan Emmett and Edwin Christie. Of the 39 composers credited in *Ryan's Mammoth Collection* (1911), a significant number were minstrel performers—banjoists, fiddlers, or clog dancers. One has only to browse through Edward L. Rice's *Monarchs of Minstrelsy* (1911), a book devoted to the biographies of minstrel performers, to conclude that these performers played mostly traditional dance music. Some of them, such as Dan Emmett, founding father of minstrelsy and the composer of "Dixie," became famous, while others, such as James Hand, remained in obscurity—their work living on principally in *Ryan's Mammoth Collection.*

It is difficult to trace the fate of *Ryan's Mammoth Collection* between 1910 and 1931, when the Howe company ceased operations. Charles Wolfe, in an excellent paper for *The Devil's Box*, picks up the Collection's history in 1940, when it was reissued by the M. M. Cole Company of Chicago as *1000 Fiddle Tunes.* He summarizes its subsequent history as follows:

> M. M. Cole was a Chicago based publishing company that had ties with radio station WLS and with Sears-Roebuck, both powerful forces in the commercialization of country music in the 1930s. Most of their songbooks featured material by one of the popular country singers like Gene Autry or Red Foley or material built around one of the emerging popular country radio shows, like the National Barn Dance or the Grand Ole' Opry. Their sales were geared to mail order, often through the *Sears-Roebuck Catalog*, and their tunebooks were of inexpensive pulp paper. When the *1,000 Fiddle Tunes* was issued in 1940, it sold for 75 cents, and was advertised as "the most complete book on the market." These factors allowed the book to get into the hands of a great many fiddlers in the South and Southwest and Midwest who had not seen Howe's original. In the years since 1940, Cole dropped most of its country songbooks, retaining only an instructional series, but kept *1,000 Fiddle Tunes* alive through a long series of reprintings. Indeed, it is still in print today(Wolfe 1987:6).

In recent years, *Ryan's Mammoth Collection* again attracted the attention of musicians and scholars when it was discovered that *1000 Fiddle Tunes* was in fact *Ryan's Mammoth Collection* rearranged. Paul Wells, at the Center for Popular Music at Middle Tennessee State University, over the course of several years has examined and cross-referenced tunes in *Ryan's Mammoth Collection* with those in other 19th-century compilations, a slow and sometimes frustrating process that promises to yield a wealth of information. My own computer-aided comparison of the 650 titles in Samuel Bayard's *Dance to the Fiddle, March to the Fife* (1982), revealed that 19 percent of the tune titles could be found in either *1000 Fiddle Tunes, Howe's Diamond School for the Violin* (1879), or *Howe's Violin School* 1879 (see Appendix 4). There are very few knowledgeable fiddlers today who have not heard of *1000 Fiddle Tunes* and many own a copy. Over the years copies have found their way into the hands of professional performers such as Paul Anatasio (formerly with "Asleep at the Wheel"), Roy Acuff, and Mark O'Connor, as well as studio musicians including Buddy Spenser, and jazz great Joe Venuti—all have used "The Fiddler's Bible" (Wolfe 1987:2). A conversation with musician John Hartford revealed that he has worn out a few copies, becoming an expert on the "Old Timey" tunes in the book. Cole's *1000 Fiddle Tunes* has also crossed the ocean. In my trips to Ireland I have seen a number of copies of the book in the homes of musicians. Just recently, prominent Irish fiddlers Tommy Peoples and Frankie Gavin both recorded tunes from the book.

The longetivity and wide appeal of Howe and Ryan's tune transcriptions contradict the generalization that fiddlers cannot read music. If this were true, then why have fiddle tune books continued to be printed over the years? Even those fiddlers who could not read music must have obtained printed tunes second-hand from fiddlers who could read or from radio shows such as the one produced by M.M. Cole on station WLS out of Chicago. In 1946 this series featured "Fiddlin' Dave" who played tunes out of "The Fiddlers Bible" on the air; a practice apparently good for business, because the station did not have to pay royalties for public domain material (Wolfe 1987:6-7).

We will never know exactly how the tunes collected and printed by Ryan and Howe influenced the American repertory. But it is clear that *Ryan's Mammoth Collection* contains a significant number of tunes that are still being played by both traditional and professional fiddlers, both North and South. Not a lot has changed; *Ryan's Mammoth Collection* helps us realize that our traditional musicians have been playing much of the same music for over 100 years.

We have seen that Ryan and Howe devoted much of their lives to collecting and publishing tune books. Anyone reading through *Ryan's Mammoth Collection* or *Howe's Musician's Omnibus* series will surely realize that Howe and Ryan both deserve recognition, along with other great collectors such as Joyce, O'Neill and Bayard, for their major contributions to the propagation and study of American and European instrumental folk music. I am sure that Ryan and Howe would agree with the words of Samuel Bayard:

> Whatever may be the changes in our traditional music, or its chances
> in the future, the fact remains that our American fifers and fiddlers
> have bequeathed to us an array of basically worthwhile melodies—
> shapely, animated, vigorous and graceful (Bayard 1982:12).

—Patrick Sky
University of North Carolina, 1995

NOTES

[1] The first U.S. copyright laws were passed in 1790 and covered books and maps. No mention was made of music. In 1831 the laws were expanded to include music (i.e., music produced and written in America). Such laws offered little protection to the author. Before 1859 a copyright could be obtained from the Secretary of State at the local court house. In 1859 all copyright deposits were transferred to the Department of the Interior and in 1865 to the Library of Congress. There was no international copyright protection until 1891 (Lichtenswanger 1980:505).

[2] In 1846 Howe published **Howe's New Boston Melodeon**, which, according to an advertisement in Howe's 1882 catalog, sold 40,000 copies over a three-year period. Next came **Howe's Accordion Preceptor** (ca.1846), which sold an estimated 100,000 copies. This success was quickly followed up by **Howe's Violin School** (ca.1846), and **The Ethiopian Glee Club** (1846) a book of minstrel tunes. There is no documentary evidence of these sales figures except the publication claims found in advertisements. Exact early publication dates are unknown. However, after 1870 most of Howe's works were eventually copyrighted (see appendix 2-3).

[3] Roorbach's **Catalogue of American Publications** (1820-1852) contains the earliest list of Howe's publications. There are nine works belonging to Ditson, who at the time did not publish **The Musician's Companion**. The catalog also shows that there were a number of other publishers involved in Howe's affairs (See appendix 2).

[4] This information was derived from a copy of **The Complete Catalogue of the Publications of Elias Howe** (1882). We know that the copyright date of **Musician's Omnibus #7** is 1882. **Ryan's Mammoth Collection** is not listed in Howe's catalog. However, an advertisement in back of the catalog states that it was "just issued" (p.28). Since **Ryan's Mammoth Collection** was not copyrighted until 1883, and since it was advertised though not listed in the 1882 catalog **Ryan's Mammoth Collection** must have been released during or before 1882 (See Appendix 7).

[5] The Library of Congress lists both **Wayside Gleanings** and **The Busy Bee**, but library personnel were unable to find either during my visit. I have not located copies of any of Ryan's later publications.

[6] This odd-sounding tune title is a corruption of "Sheela na Gig" the name for one of the Celtic fertility Goddesses, whose grotesque effigy can be found over the doorways of many ancient stone churches throughout Ireland and England.

Bibliography

Adams, George, ed. 1840-1900. *Directory of the City of Boston*. Boston: George Adams.

American Catalog of Authors and Titles. 1866-1910. New York: New York Publishers Weekly.

Ayars Christine. 1937. "Elias Howe." in *Contributions to the Art of Music in America by the Music Industries of Boston*. Pp.12-16 and pp.260-261. New York: The H.W. Wilson Company.

Bayard, Samuel P. 1982. *Dance to the Fiddle, March to the Fife*. University Park: Pennsylvania State University Press.

Board of Music Trade of the United States of America. [1870] 1973. *The Complete Catalogue of Sheet Music and Musical Works*. New York: Reprint. De Capo.

Breathnach, Breandan. 1971. *Folk Music and Dances of Ireland*. Dublin: Mercier Press.

Bunting, Edward. 1796. *A General Collection of the Ancient Music of Ireland*. London: Hodges and Smith.

Chase, Gilbert. 1987. *America's Music*. Chicago: University of Illinois Press.

Cole, M. M.,ed. 1940. *One Thousand Fiddle Tunes*. Chicago: M. M. Cole Co.

Dichter, Cole and Harry and Elliot Shapiro. [1941] 1977. *The Handbook of Early American Sheet Music 1768-1889*. New York: Dover Press. Reprint.

Dwight, John S., ed. [1852-1881] 1967. *Dwight's Journal of Music*. 41 Vols. Vol.6, p.118. Jan.13, 1855. New York: Reprint, Johnson Reprint Co. Arno Press.

Dyer, Gen. Richard. 1893. *The Annual Report of the Adjutant General*. Providence, R.I: Freeman and Sons.

"Elias Howe Esq." New England Historical and Genealogical Register. 1895. p.480. Boston: New England Historical and Genealogical Society.

Epstein, Dena J. 1973. "Introduction." *The Complete Catalogue of Sheet Music and Musical Works*. Pp.v- xx. New York: Da Capo.

French, Jacob. 1779 *The New American Melody*. Boston: Author.

Goertzen, Chris. 1983. Billy in the Lowground: A History of An American Instrumental Folk Tune. Ph.D. Diss. University of Illinois.

Goldstein, Kenneth. 1992. Personal telephone conversation.

Herndon, Richard. 1892. "Elias Howe Jr." *Boston of Today*. ed. Edwin Bacon. Boston: Post Publishing Company, pp.265-266.

Holyoke, Samuel. ca.1800. *The Instrumental Assistant.* New York: Author

Howe, Elias. 1872. *The Complete Catalog of The Publications of Elias Howe*. Boston: Howe.

____. ca.1842 *The Musician's Companion*. Boston: Howe.

____. 1864-1883. *The Musician's Omnibus*, Vols. 1-7. Boston:Howe.

____. n.d. *Howe's One Thousand Reels and Jigs*. Boston: Howe.

____. n.d. *Howe's New Boston Melodeon*. Boston: Howe.

____. ca.1870. *Howe's Accordion Preceptor*. Boston: Howe.

____. ca.1846. *Howe's Violin school*. Boston: Howe.

____. ca.1877. *The Ethiopian Glee Club*. Boston: Howe.

Joyce, P.W. 1873. *Ancient Irish Music*. Dublin: Gill and Son.

Lamb, Andrew. 1980. "Popular Music." In *The New Grove Dictionary of Music and Musicians*. ed. Stanley Sadie. Vol.15, pp.87-97. New York: Macmillan.

Lichtenswanger, William. 1980. "Copyright." in *The New Grove's Dictionary of American Music,* ed. Stanley Sadie. Vol.1, pp.505-509. New York: Macmillan.

McKay, David P. 1980. "William Billings" in *The New Grove's Dictionary of Music and Musicians.* ed. Stanley Sadie.Vol.2, pp. 703-705 New York: Macmillan.

Odell, George C. D. 1927-1949. *Annals of the New York Stage*. New York: Columbia University press.

O'Neill, Francis. [1922] 1980. *Waifs and Strays of Gaelic Melody,* enlarged edition. Reprint. Dublin: Mercier Press.

____. [1903] 1971. *Music of Ireland-1800 tunes*. New York: Reprint. New Jersey: Dan Collins.

Petrie, George. 1855, *The Petrie Collection of the Ancient Music of Ireland*. London: Boosey and Co.

Playford, John. 1654. *An Introduction To The Skill O f Music*. London: Playford.

____. 1651. *The English Dancing Master*. London: Author.

Reed, Daniel. 1785. *American Singing Book*. New Haven: Author

Rice, Edward Leroy. 1911. *Monarchs of Minstrelsy: from "Daddy" Rice to Date*. New York: Kenny Publishing Co.

Riley, Edward. [1814-1824] 1979. *Riley's Flute Melodies*, 2 Vols. Reprint. New York: Da Capo Press.

Rippin, Edward N. 1980. "Pianoforte." In *The New Dictionary of Music and Musicians*. ed. Stanley Sadie. Vol.14,pp. 683-714. New York: Macmillan.

Roorbach, O. A. 1849, 1852. *Catalogue of American Publications,* 2 Vols. New York: Putnam.

Ryan ,William B. Ryan. 1883. *Ryan's Mammoth Collection*. Boston: Elias Howe.

Sadie, Stanley.,ed. 1980. *The New Grove Dictionary of American Music*. 4 Vols. New York: Macmillan.

____. 1980. *The New Grove Dictionary of Music and Musicians*. 20 Vols. New York: Macmillan.

Sears Catalog. 1906, 1902. Chicago: Sears Roebuck and Co.

Smith, Ronnie L. 1980. "Joseph Carr" In *The New Grove's Dictionary of Music and Musicians*, ed. Stanley Sadie. Vol.3, p. 822. New York: Macmillan.

Temple, J. H. 1887. *History of Framingham Massachusetts*. Framingham: Town of Framingham.

Tompkins, Eugene. 1908. *The History of the BostonTheatre: 1854-1901*. Boston: Houghton Mifflin Co. William B. Ryan. "Obituary" *Boston Globe*, Dec. 7, 1910. p. 8.

William Bradbury Ryan."Obituary" *Boston EveningTranscript*, Dec. 7, 1910. p. 4.

Wolfe, Charles. 1987. "The Fiddler's Bible: A Brief History" *The Devils Box* 21(4):37-48.

Wolfe, Richard. 1964. *Secular Music In America 1801-1825*.3 Vols. New York: New York Public Library.

Woodbury, August. 1875. *The Second Rhode Island Regiment*. Providence : Valpey, Angell and Co.

Patrick Sky

Patricky Sky is a noted folk musician, author, and songwriter. He plays the Irish Uilleann pipes, was one of the founders of Green Linnett Records and has been involved in folk music for over thirty years. He has a Masters degree in folklore from the University of North Carolina at Chapel Hill, where he resides with his wife, Cathy and son Liam.

Patrick Sky, for those of you unfamiliar with the '60s has been involved with playing his music and performing for over thirty years. He has sold out Carnagie Hall, and played for standing room only all over the United States, Canada and Europe. Among many of his major appearances are: The Montreal Expo, The Central Park Music Festival and Town Hall in New York, and the Royal Festival Hall in London. Most recently: The Philadelphia Folk Festival, The Winnipeg Festival and many, many clubs.

Patrick has seven solo albums to his credit....two on Vanguard records, "PATRICK SKY" AND "A HARVEST OF GENTLE CLANG", are his first recordings made in the mid sixties. His latest album on the Shanachie label is called "THROUGH A WINDOW" and is a selection of his favorite songs from that era. In addition, he has produced over 24 albums for other artists such as the Mississippi John Hurt, Paul Geremia, Mick Maloney, Rosalie Sorrels and Seamus Ennis, to name a few. He was the founder of Green Linnett Records, wrote film scores for McGraw Hill, and is the author of "A MANUAL FOR THE UILLEANN PIPES" (the most extensive book ever written on the subject). At present he is the president of Skylark Productions, Inc. and is co-author of "THE DIXIE DEWDROP" the first musical ever written about Uncle Dave Macon.

For the last few years, Patrick lived in Ireland where he learned to play the Uilleann Pipes from two of the oldest masters, Seamus Ennis and Tommy Reck. Patrick is deeply involved in bringing Irish music to the United States. It was Patrick who gave Liam O'Flynn his stage experience when he hired him in 1970 as his opening act.

His new stage show combines old songs, new songs; traditional, original and modern; he plays Irish music on the Uilleann Pipes, and a mixed bag of tunes on the whistle, flute and guitar. His salty stories and jokes are as bad as ever—the audience loves it! To quote BILLBOARD "All purpose is the word for Patrick Sky. He sings, plays excellent guitar and pipes, and even better tells horrible stories, and the combination of these makes him a most engaging performer".

Patrick Sky

BLODGETT'S—REEL.

"FIRE HIM OUT"—REEL.

KELTON'S—REEL.
Or "Pig Town Fling."

BRAZEN MASK—REEL.

WITCH OF THE WAVE—REEL.

WELCOME HERE AGAIN—REEL.

THE SCOTCH PATRIOT'S—REEL.

'NEATH THE MOONLIGHT—REEL.

TULLOCHGORUM—REEL.

SCOTCH.

WHIDDON'S FAVORITE—REEL.

BANJO—REEL.

IRISH - AMERICAN—REEL.

OUR BOYS'—REEL.

INMAN LINE—REEL.

H. F. WILLIAMS.

JUDY'S—REEL.

PADDY HANDLY'S GOOSE—REEL.

ARKANSAS TRAVELLER—REEL.

GAME COCK—REEL.

CAMERONIAN—REEL.

JUDY MALEY'S—REEL.

PADDY THE PIPER—REEL.

THE RAKISH HIGHLANDER—REEL.

PARNELL'S—REEL.

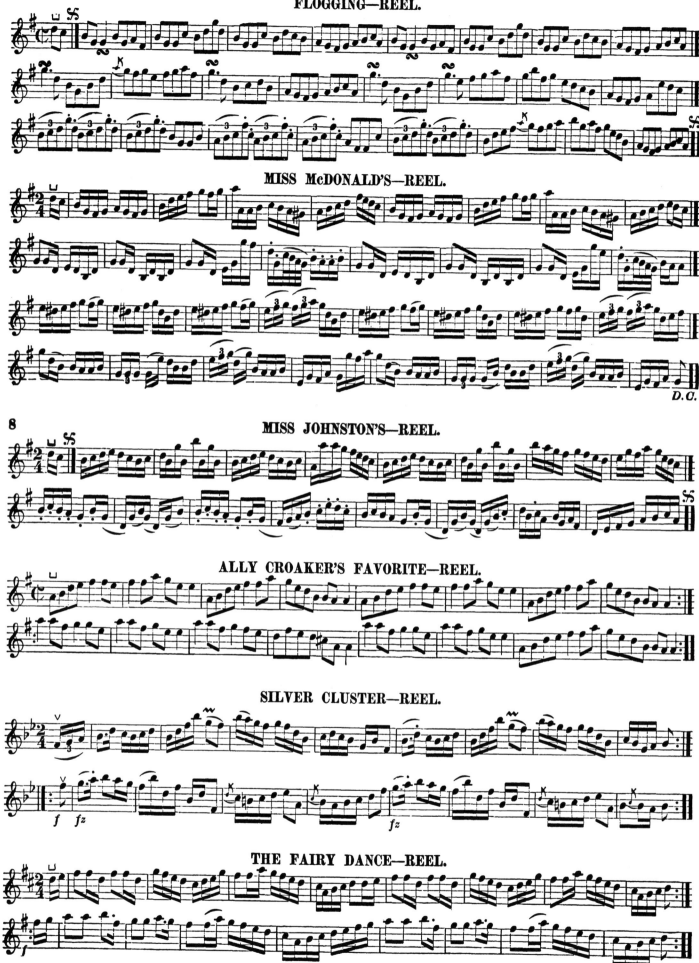

FLOGGING—REEL.

MISS McDONALD'S—REEL.

MISS JOHNSTON'S—REEL.

ALLY CROAKER'S FAVORITE—REEL.

SILVER CLUSTER—REEL.

THE FAIRY DANCE—REEL.

THREE MERRY SISTERS—REEL.

THE PRIMROSE LASS—REEL.

BELLES OF TIPPERARY—REEL.

LORD GORDON'S—REEL.

JENNY DANGED THE WEAVER—REEL.

SALAMANCA—REEL.

THE BOYNE HUNT—REEL.

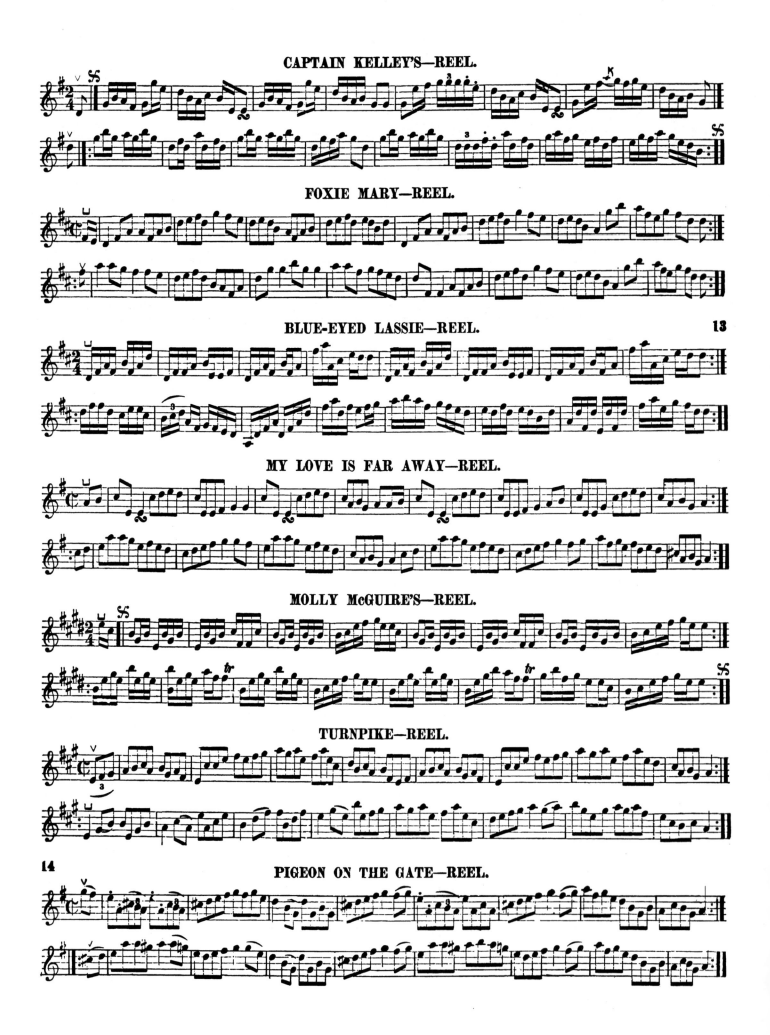

CAPTAIN KELLEY'S—REEL.

FOXIE MARY—REEL.

BLUE-EYED LASSIE—REEL.

13

MY LOVE IS FAR AWAY—REEL.

MOLLY McGUIRE'S—REEL.

TURNPIKE—REEL.

14

PIGEON ON THE GATE—REEL.

ABITHA MUGGINS' FAVORITE—REEL.

DUBLIN LASSES—REEL.

BLACKBERRY BLOSSOM—REEL.

KISS ME, JOE—REEL.

15

THE CUP OF TEA—REEL.

I'M OVER YOUNG TO MARRY YET—REEL.

MILL-TOWN MAID—REEL.

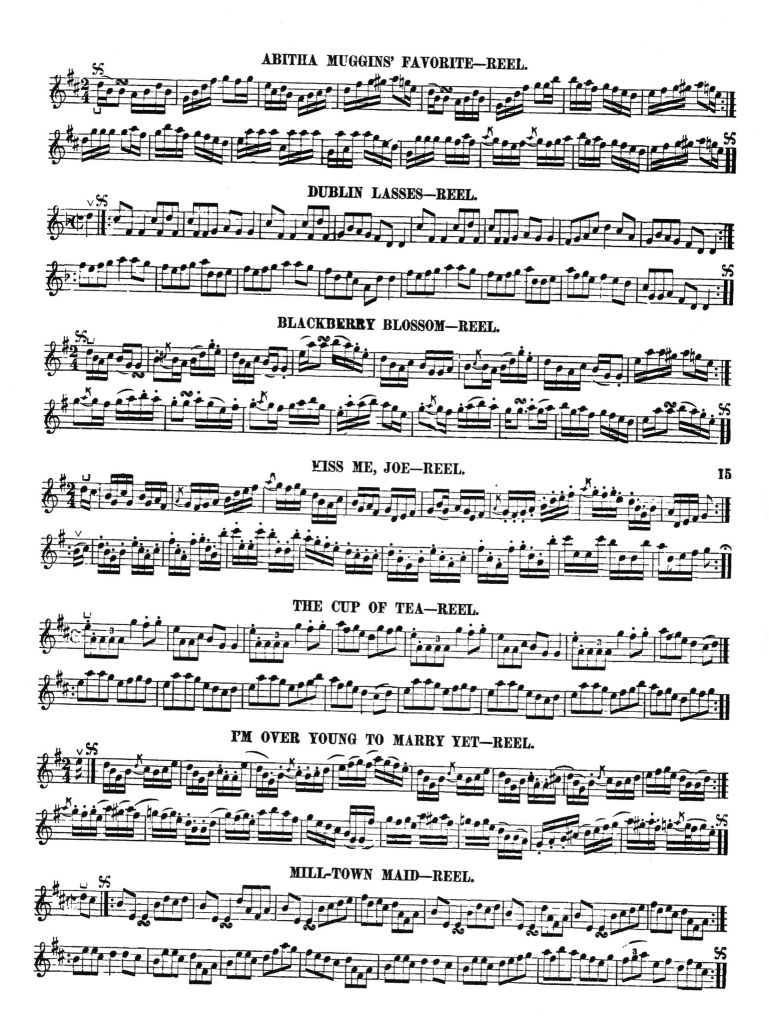

DARK HAIRED LASS—REEL.

BRIDE OF KILDARE—REEL.

TERENCE'S RAMBLE—REEL.

MY LOVE IS IN AMERICA—REEL.

MAGGIE PICKING COCKELS—REEL.

FAREWELL TO ERIN—REEL.

TEMPERANCE—REEL.

EYES RIGHT—REEL.

THE ROVING BACHELOR—REEL.

GOOD-BYE, SWEETHEART—REEL.

REILLY'S—REEL.

ROSE - BUD—REEL.
Or "Mountain Ranger Hornpipe."

CHARMING MOLLIE'S--REEL.

BLIND NORRY'S—REEL.

THE BANKS OF ENVERNESS—REEL.

LIMERICK LASSES—REEL.

KITTY CLOVER'S—REEL.

OH, GANG WITH ME TO YON TOWN—REEL.

THE ROWAN TREE—REEL.

SPIRVINS' FANCY—REEL.

THE LADUS—REEL.

HUMORS OF TUFTS STREET—REEL.

LADY MONTGOMERY'S—REEL.

BRAES OF DUMBLANE—REEL.

BENNETT'S FAVORITE—REEL.

LEAGUE AND SLASHER—REEL.

LADY EDMONTON'S—REEL.

OLD MAIDS OF GALWAY—REEL.

WIDE AWAKE—REEL.

MISS CORBETT'S—REEL.

D.C.

FLOWERS OF CAHIRCIVEEN—REEL.

LADY FORBE'S—REEL.

THE JOLLY TINKER'S—REEL.

BUCKLEY'S FAVORITE—REEL.

SHIPS ARE SAILING—REEL.

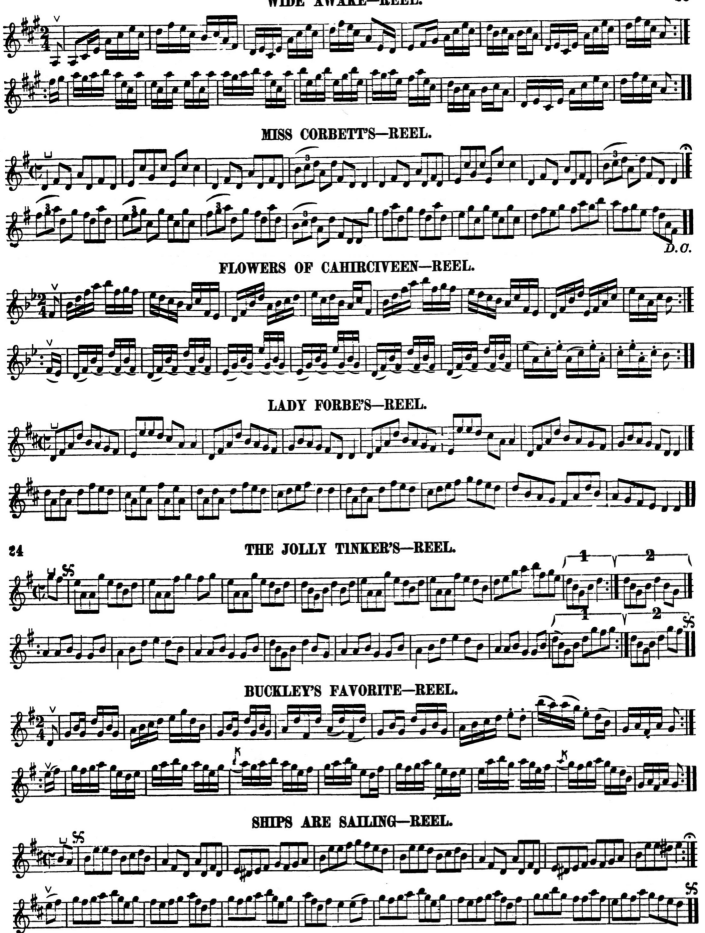

MISS BROWN'S—REEL.

LAVEN'S FAVORITE—REEL.

BROOKLYN LASSES—REEL.

THE MILLER'S MAID—REEL.

NIEL GOW'S—REEL.

D.C.

THE BOSTON—REEL.

MAY - POLE—REEL.

D.C.

CAPE COD—REEL.

HOBB'S FAVORITE—REEL.

THE PIPER'S LASS—REEL.

27

SARATOGA—REEL.

QUEEN'S GUARDS—REEL.

THE JOLLY CLAM-DIGGER'S—REEL.

28

THE WIND UP—REEL.

TEETOTALERS'—REEL.

FILL UP THE BOWL—REEL.

THE MASONS' CAP—REEL.

BLACKWATER—REEL.

29

ONCE UPON MY CHEEK—REEL.

MORTON'S—REEL.

ROSE OF THE VALLEY—REEL.

CONNEMARA'S PET—REEL.

THE BONNIE LAD—REEL.

FIVE LEAVED CLOVER—REEL.

NED KENDALL'S FAVORITE—REEL.

THE LAVENDER GIRL—REEL.

THE TIN-WARE LASS—REEL.

DAFFY, DON'T YOU—REEL.

GREEN FIELDS OF AMERICA—REEL.

RISING SUN—REEL.

DIAMOND—REEL.

JOHNNY'S GONE TO FRANCE—REEL.

CHARMING KATY'S—REEL.

FIRE-FLY—REEL.

HONEY-MOON—REEL.

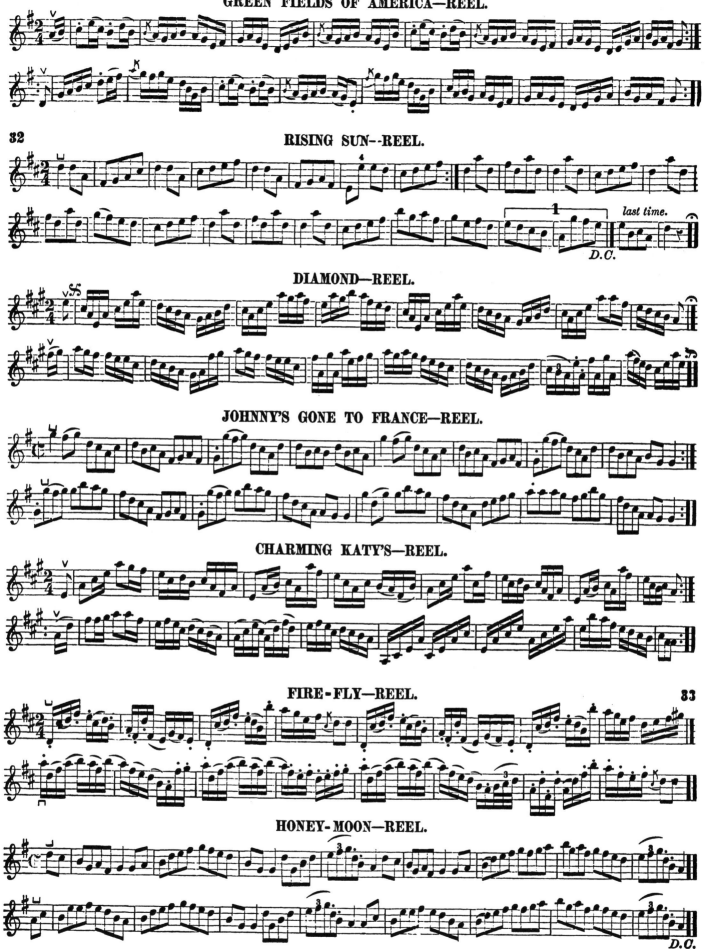

41

ARBANA—REEL.

RAT-CATCHER'S—REEL.

84

LORD DALHOUSIE'S—REEL.

GREEN HILLS OF TYROL—REEL.

THE DEVIL AMONG THE TAILORS—REEL.

D.C.

REED'S FAVORITE—REEL.

THE COUNTESS OF LOUDEN'S—REEL.

35

SMITH'S DELIGHT—REEL.

JENNY'S BABY—REEL.

HIT OR MISS—REEL.

36

FROM NIGHT TILL MORN—REEL.

CORPORAL CASEY'S FANCY—REEL.

MISS CAMPBELL'S—REEL.

"YOU BET"—REEL.

JAS. HAND.

SYNTHA—REEL.
JAS. HAND.

KISS THE BRIDE—REEL.

LARDNERS'—REEL.

SLEEPY MAGGY—REEL.

CORKONIAN—REEL.

CONGRESS PARK—REEL.

TWO FORTY—REEL.

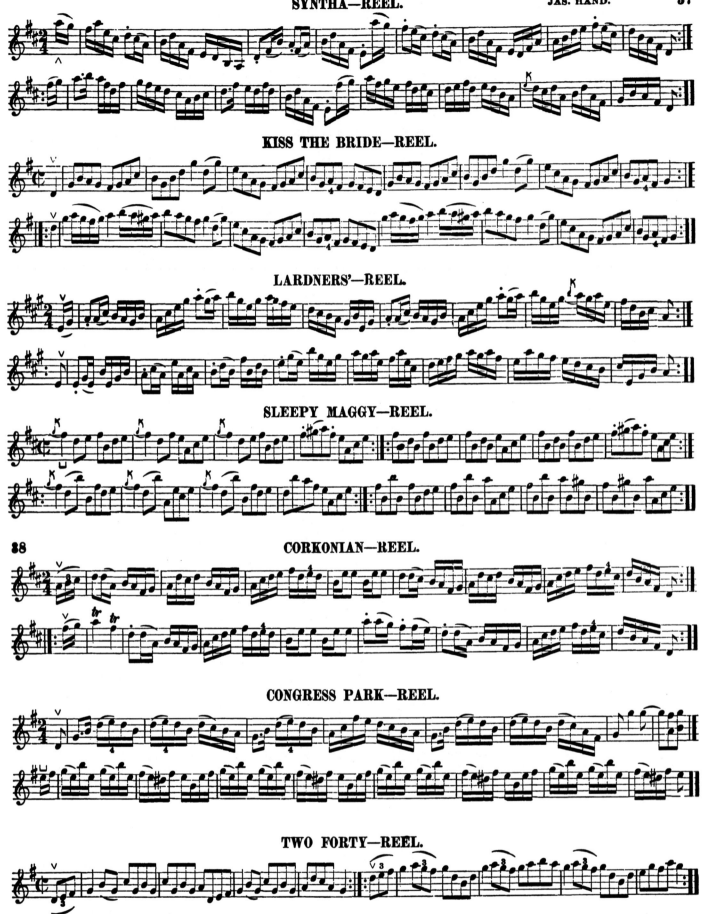

LEAP YEAR—REEL.

"WAKE UP, SUSAN"—REEL.

ALL THE WAY TO GALWAY—REEL.

GREEN GROW THE RUSHES O—REEL.

FLOWERS OF EDINBURG—REEL.

PEELERS JACKET—REEL.

WIND THAT SHAKES THE BARLEY—REEL.

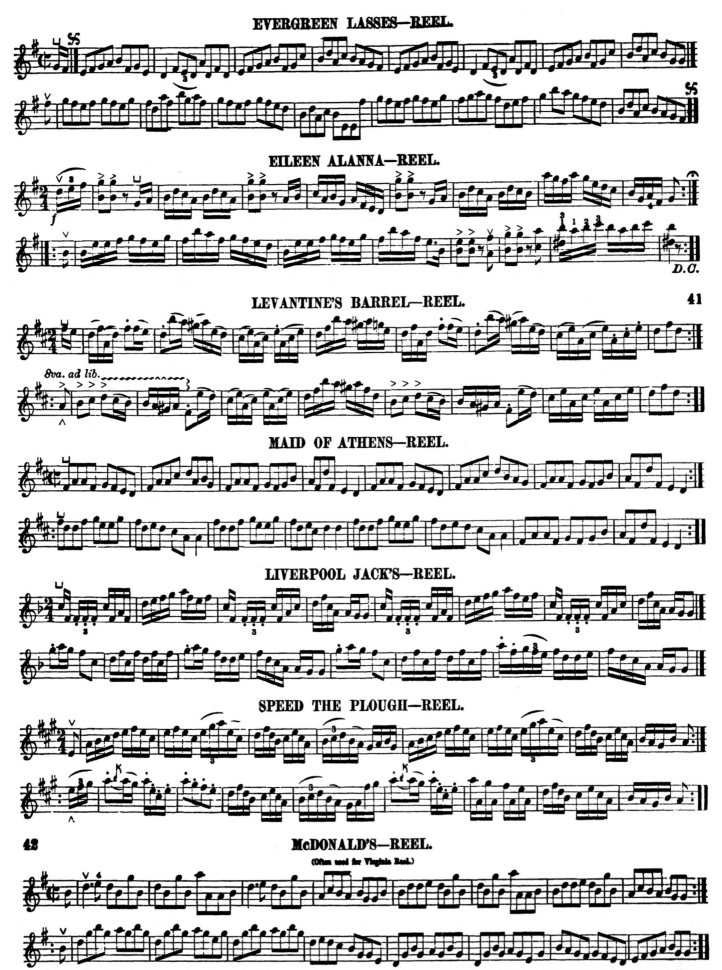

EVERGREEN LASSES—REEL.

EILEEN ALANNA—REEL.

LEVANTINE'S BARREL—REEL.

MAID OF ATHENS—REEL.

LIVERPOOL JACK'S—REEL.

SPEED THE PLOUGH—REEL.

McDONALD'S—REEL.
(Often used for Virginia Reel.)

VIRGINIA REEL. First lady and foot gent, forward (meet each other) and return to places.—First gent and foot lady same—First lady and foot gent, forward, turn with right hands, back to places.—First gent and foot lady same—First lady and foot gent, forward, turn with left hands, back to places.—First gent and foot lady same—First lady and foot gent, forward, turn with both hands, back to places.—First gent and foot lady same—First lady and foot gent, forward, back to back.—First gent and foot lady same—[SELDOM USED.] First couple give right hands, left hands to opposite, (so on to foot of set) up centre with partner to places.—March: ladies to right, gents to left, all up the centre. First couple down centre and stop.

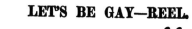

LET'S BE GAY—REEL.

FIRST NIGHT IN LEADVILLE—REEL.

THE ALHAMBRA—REEL.

KILKENNY BOYS'—REEL.

43

PADDY ON THE TURNPIKE—REEL.

THE KEEL-ROW—REEL.
(Or TWIN SISTERS.)

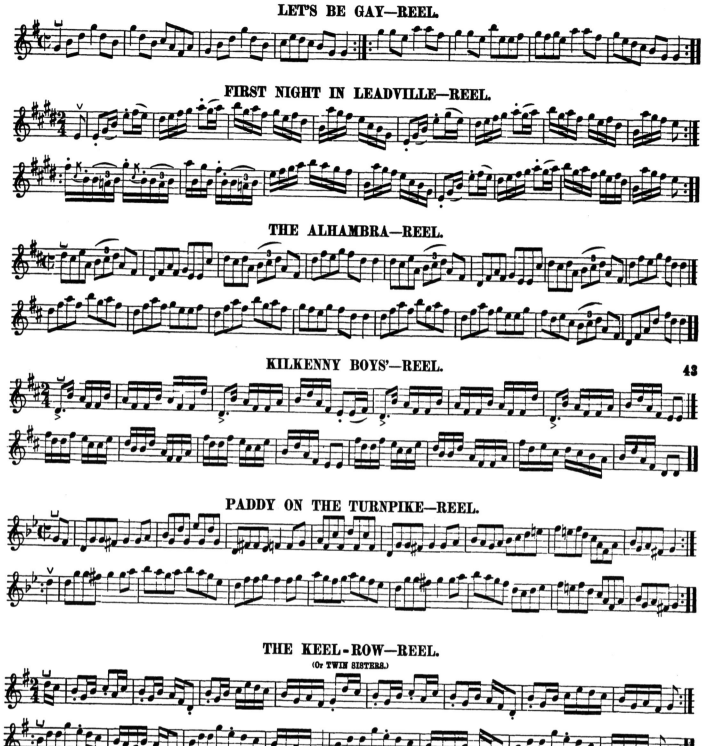

TWIN SISTERS.—First two ladies join hands, chassa across. [same time] First two gents chassa across, outside singly, join hands, chassa back, [same time] two ladies return outside.—First couple down the centre, back, cast off, right and left. [Next two ladies, etc.

ECHOES FROM FOREST GARDEN—REEL.

SPIRIT OF 1880—REEL.

OLD ZIP COON—REEL.

OLD ZIP COON.—First couple down the outside and back up the centre, [second couple down the centre and back up the outside at same time.] First couple down the centre and back up the outside, [second couple down the outside and back up the centre at same time.] First and second couples down the centre together, back.—First couple cast off, right and left four.

SMASH THE WINDOWS—REEL.

THE GRAND SPY—REEL.

SPIT-FIRE—REEL.

MISS GAY'S—REEL.

PANTOMIME—REEL.

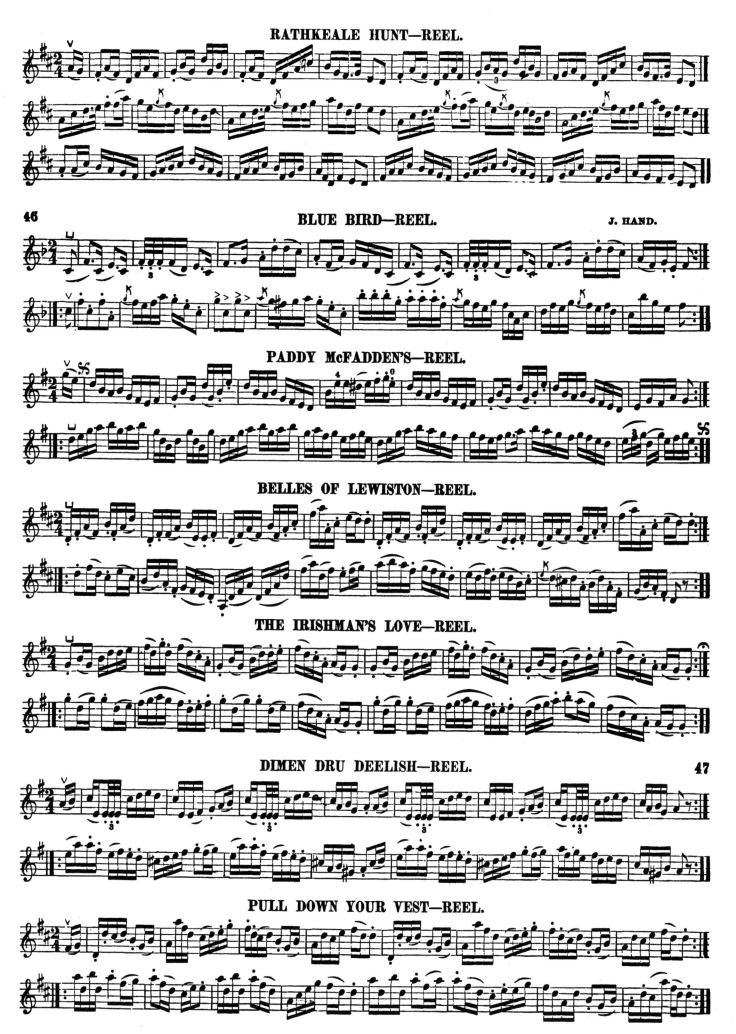

RATHKEALE HUNT—REEL.

BLUE BIRD—REEL.

J. HAND.

PADDY McFADDEN'S—REEL.

BELLES OF LEWISTON—REEL.

THE IRISHMAN'S LOVE—REEL.

DIMEN DRU DEELISH—REEL.

PULL DOWN YOUR VEST—REEL.

HALF - PENNY—REEL.

LADY WALPOLE'S—REEL.
(Often called Lady Washington's Reel—or Boston Fancy.)

LADY WALPOLE'S REEL.—First couple cross over and balance, turn same; down the centre with partners, and back, (each remain on the others side of set until the foot) Ladies' chain.—half promenade, half right and left to places.

WATERLOO—REEL.

McGUFFUM'S—REEL.

WINNIE GREEN'S FAVORITE—REEL.

D.C.

STICK IT IN THE ASHES—REEL.

BEN LOWRY'S—REEL.

WHO MADE YOUR BREECHES?—REEL.

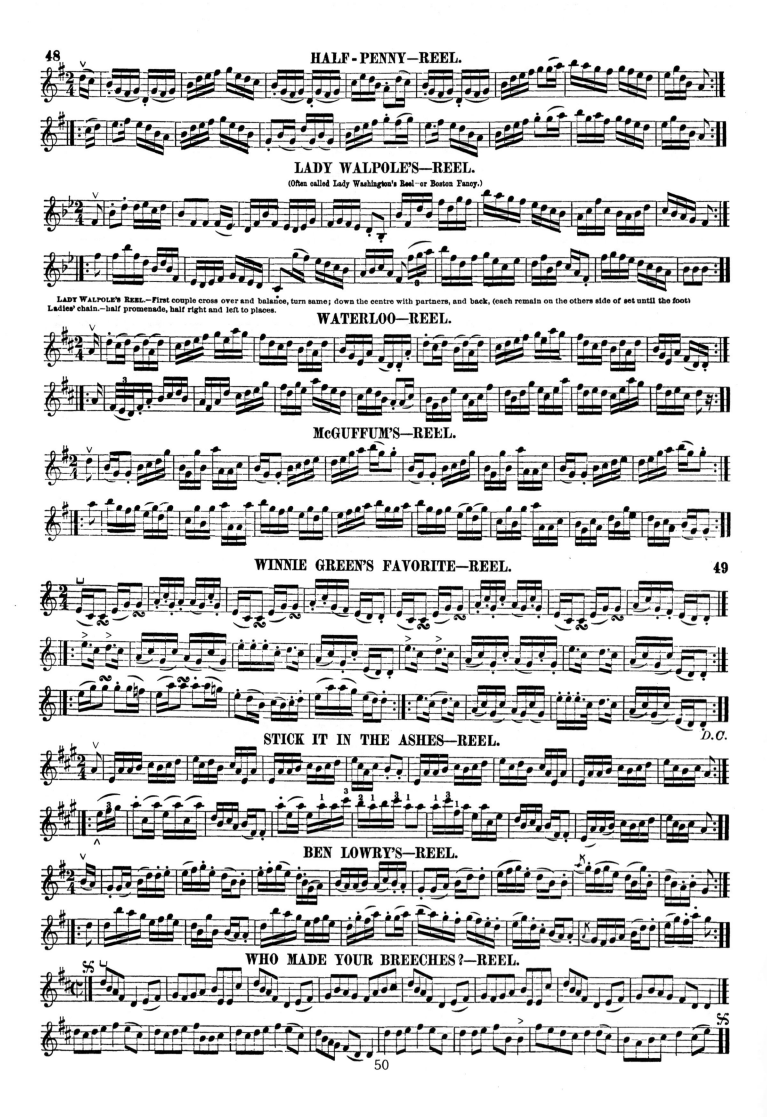

NEW WEDDING—REEL.

D.C.

PADDY ON THE RAILROAD—REEL.

50

COME, TILL THE BOTTLE-HOUSE—REEL.

DONEGALL BOYS'—REEL.

OLD BACHELORS'—REEL.

WITHIN A MILE OF CLONBUR—REEL.

HIGHLAND SKIP—REEL.

51

D.C.

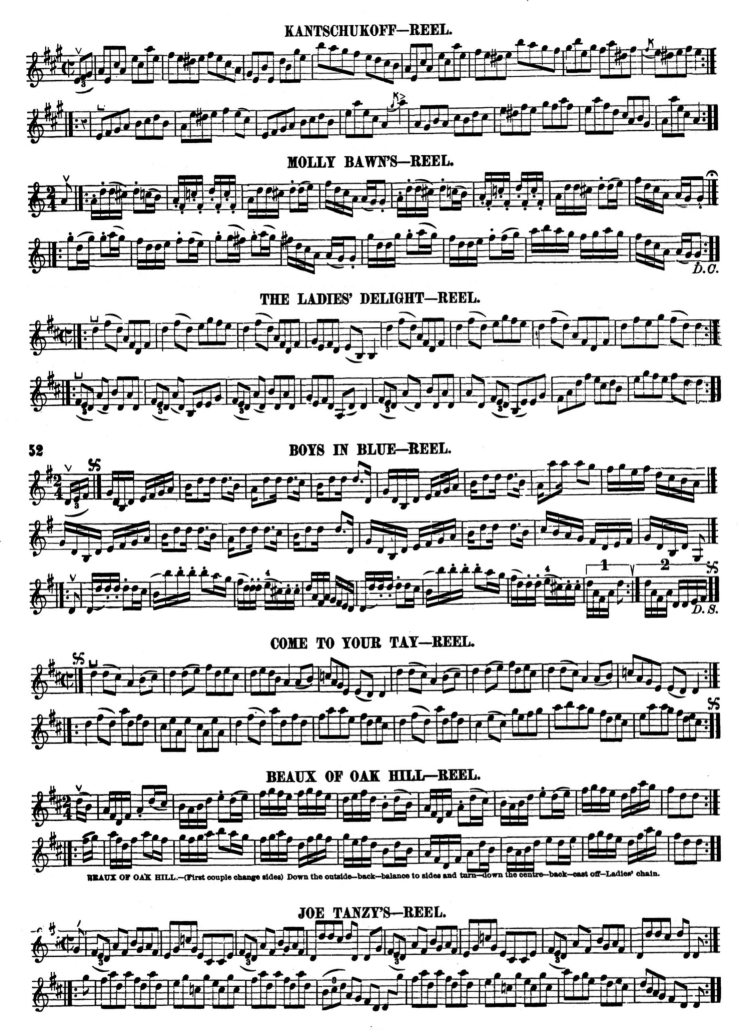

KANTSCHUKOFF—REEL.

MOLLY BAWN'S—REEL.

THE LADIES' DELIGHT—REEL.

BOYS IN BLUE—REEL.

COME TO YOUR TAY—REEL.

BEAUX OF OAK HILL—REEL.

BEAUX OF OAK HILL.—(First couple change sides) Down the outside—back—balance to sides and turn—down the centre—back—cast off—Ladies' chain.

JOE TANZY'S—REEL.

CALE SMITH'S PASTIME—REEL.

NEW LINE—REEL.

BOY IN THE GAP—REEL.

THE JOLLY SEVEN—REEL.

54

FLOWERS OF ST. PETERSBURG—REEL.

THE BOSTON BOYS'—REEL.

OLD SPORT—REEL.

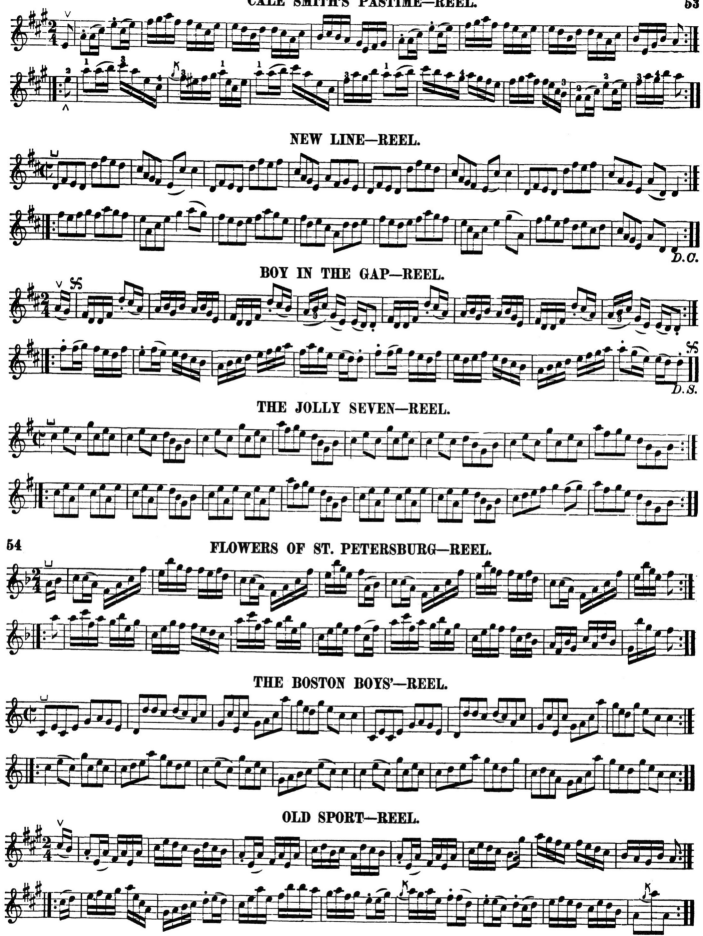

THE LONDON LASSES—REEL.

MISS GUNNING'S FANCY—REEL.

AROUND THE WORLD—REEL.

MISS HORGAN'S—REEL.

HUMOURS OF ROCKSTOWN—REEL.

THE MAGIC SLIPPER—REEL.

THE DEVIL'S DREAM—REEL.

DEVIL'S DREAM. *(Form in sets of six couples.)*—First couple down the outside and back, (foot couples up the centre and back at same time) First couple down the centre, back, cast off, (foot couples up the outside and back at the same time) Ladies' chain (first four)—Right and left.

THE RIVAL—REEL.

MY LOVE IS ON THE OCEAN—REEL.

JENNY'S WEDDING—REEL.   J. HAND.   57

MISS McCLOUD'S—REEL.

BOSTON RATTLERS'—REEL.

QUEEN OF CLUB'S—REEL.

58   PAT CARNEY'S—REEL.

"CHEESE IT!"—REEL.

OLD JOE SIFE'S—REEL.

DAN BACKUS' FAVORITE—REEL.

DANDY MIKE'S—REEL.

59

FLOWERS OF LIMERICK—REEL.

OPERA—REEL.

OPERA REEL. (*Form in sets of six couples.*)—First couple balance, down the centre to the foot of set. Second couple balance down the centre to foot of set. Right and left 4 at the foot, both couples up the centre. First couple down the outside and remain at the foot.

CLEMENS'—REEL.

HARRISON'S CELEBRATED—REEL.

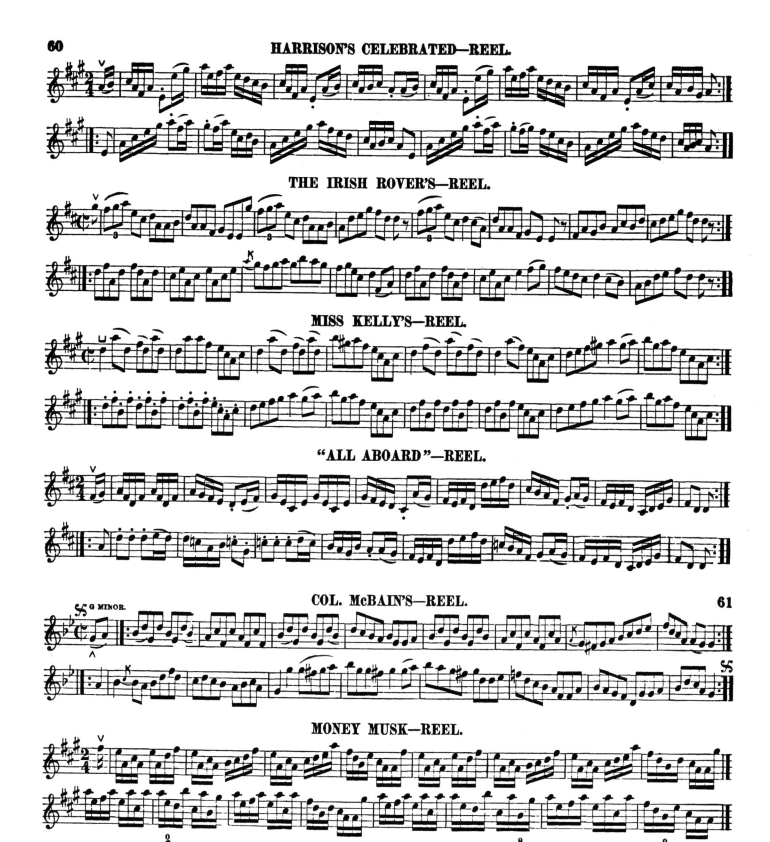

THE IRISH ROVER'S—REEL.

MISS KELLY'S—REEL.

"ALL ABOARD"—REEL.

COL. McBAIN'S—REEL.

MONEY MUSK—REEL.

VARIATION FIRST.—*To second strain, ad lib.*

VARIATION SECOND.—*To second strain, ad lib.*

MONEY MUSK.—First couple join right hands and swing once and a half round, go below second couple, forward and back six. First couple give right hands, swing three quarters round (to inside of set) forward and back six, first couple give right hands, swing to place, right and left four.

PADDY MILES' FRICASSEE—REEL.

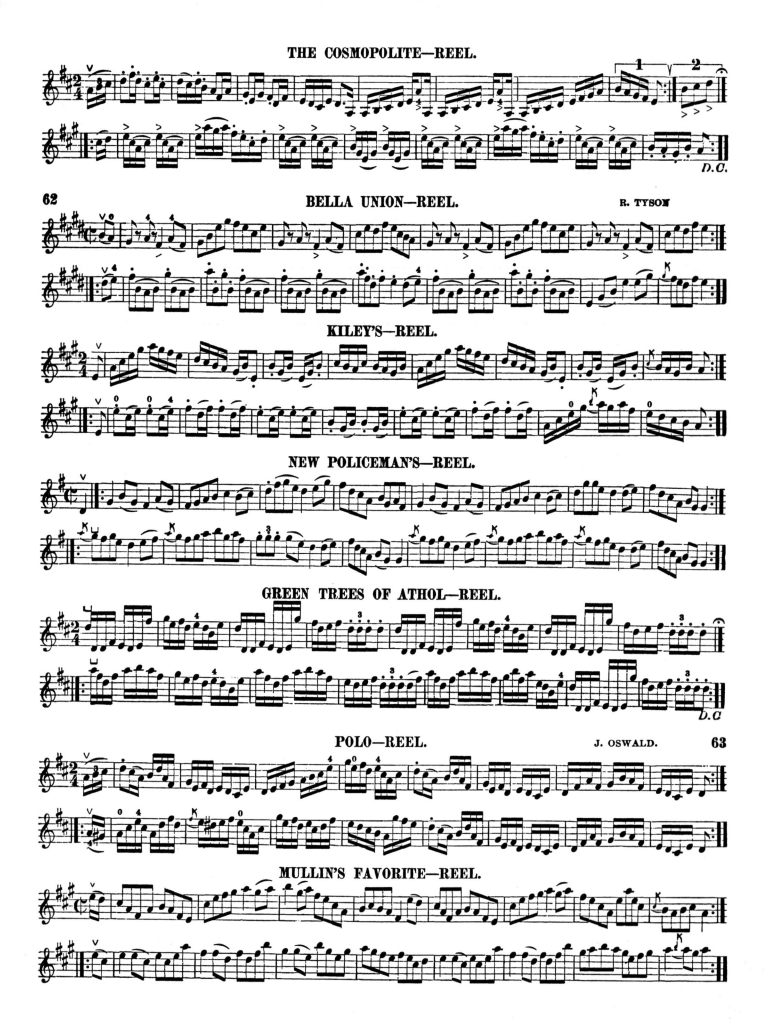

THE COSMOPOLITE—REEL.

BELLA UNION—REEL.

R. TYSON

KILEY'S—REEL.

NEW POLICEMAN'S—REEL.

GREEN TREES OF ATHOL—REEL.

POLO—REEL.

J. OSWALD.

MULLIN'S FAVORITE—REEL.

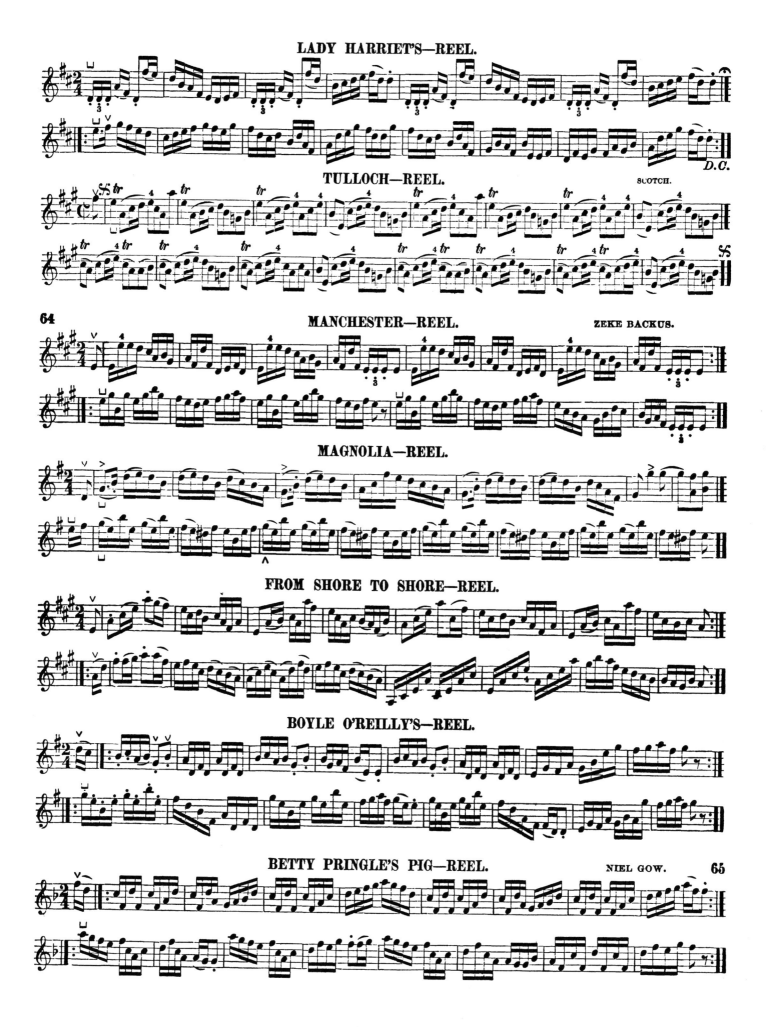

LADY HARRIET'S—REEL.

TULLOCH—REEL.

SCOTCH.

64

MANCHESTER—REEL.

ZEKE BACKUS.

MAGNOLIA—REEL.

FROM SHORE TO SHORE—REEL.

BOYLE O'REILLY'S—REEL.

BETTY PRINGLE'S PIG—REEL.

NIEL GOW.

65

EVANSVILLE—REEL.

RUSTIC—REEL.

RUSTIC REEL. *Each gent. has two partners. Form as for Spanish Dance.* Each gent. chassa out with right hand lady opposite, and back; chassa out with left hand lady opposite, and back. All forward and back—pass through to next couples.

LADY ELGIN'S COURTSHIP—REEL.

66

PEEP O' DAY—REEL.

N. GOW.

THE GREEN FLAG IS FLYING—REEL.

BRIGHTEST EYES'—REEL.

AFTER THE HARE—REEL.

A MINOR.

CROSS ROAD—REEL.

NICODEMUS JOHNSON'S—REEL.

MISS PLAUDY'S—REEL.

MARQUIS HANSLEY'S—REEL.

SCOTCH.

FLAT FOOT—REEL.

INIMITABLE—REEL.

As performed by E. CHRISTIE.

KITTY CLYDE'S—REEL.

LUCY CAMPBELL'S—REEL.

SCOTCH.

YELLOW HAIR'D LADDIE—REEL.

SCOTCH.

BLUFF—REEL.

G. L. TRACY.

71

LARRY DOWNS'—REEL.

LADY JANE GRAY'S—REEL.

PRIDE OF THE BALL—REEL.

72

HIPPODROME—REEL.

G. L. TRACY.

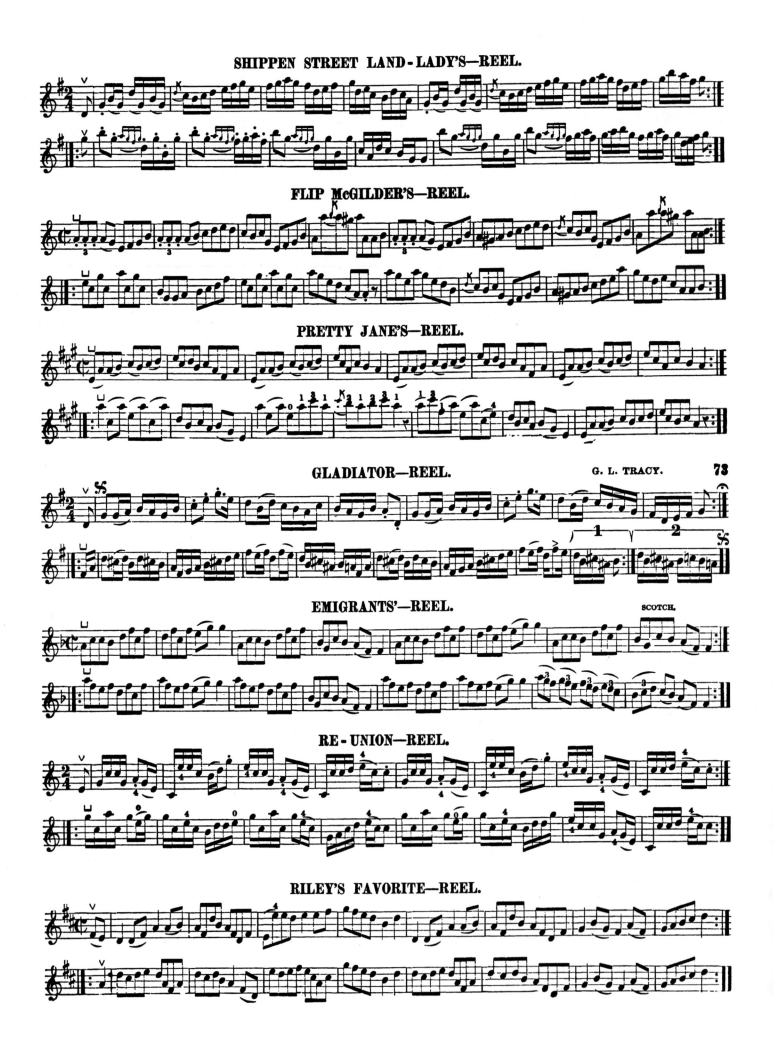

TELEPHONE—REEL.

As performed by C. W. KNOWLTON.

THE YORKSHIRE BITE—REEL.

NEW YORK—REEL.

BELLES OF OMAHA—REEL.

TOM DEERING'S RAMBLES—REEL.

E. CHRISTIE.

DOMINION—REEL.

PULASKI GUARDS'—REEL.

MARDI GRAS—REEL.

LITTLE DUKE'S—REEL.

FLIRTATION—REEL.

78

POST HORN—REEL.

FRANK LIVINGSTON.

JACK SMITH'S FAVORITE—REEL.

ACACIA—REEL.

PEGGY WHIFFLE'S—REEL.

OSTINELLI'S—REEL.

79

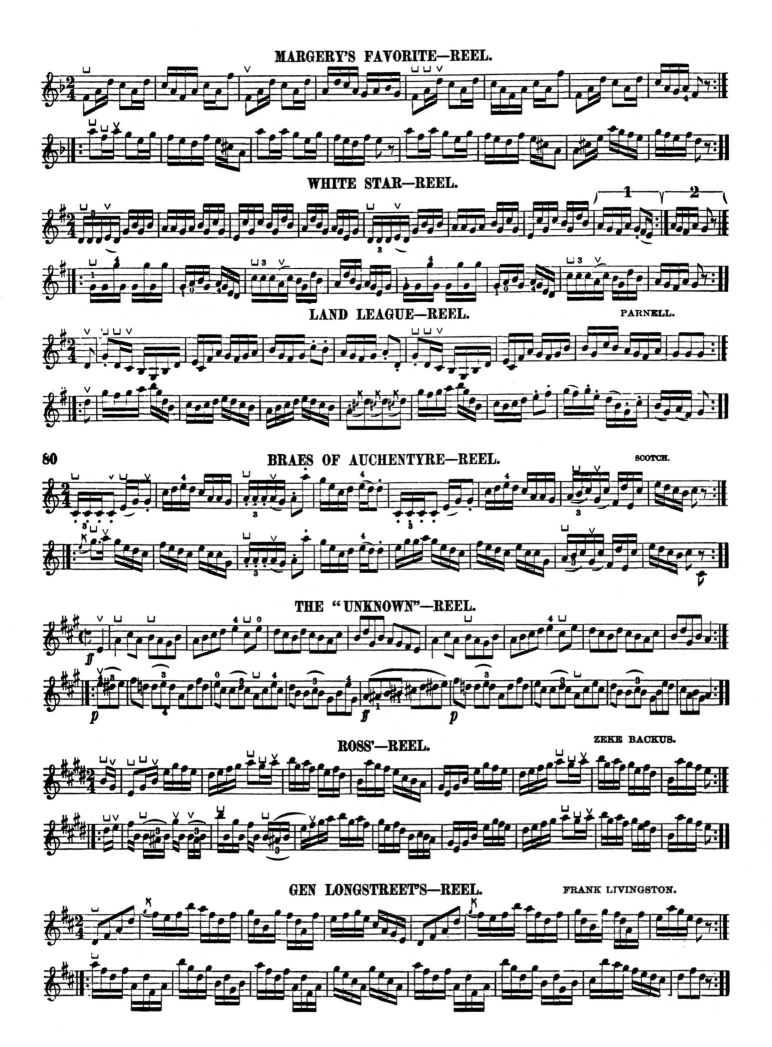

MARGERY'S FAVORITE—REEL.

WHITE STAR—REEL.

LAND LEAGUE—REEL.   PARNELL.

80   BRAES OF AUCHENTYRE—REEL.   SCOTCH.

THE "UNKNOWN"—REEL.

ROSS'—REEL.   ZEKE BACKUS.

GEN LONGSTREET'S—REEL.   FRANK LIVINGSTON.

CALIFORNIA—REEL.

FRANK LIVINGSTON.

PINK EYED LASSIE—REEL.

SUKEY BIDS ME—REEL.

SCOTCH.

GREETING TO IRELAND—REEL.

BELLE OF BOSTON—REEL.

E. CHRISTIE.

D.C.

MAGUINNIS' DELIGHT—REEL.

"GOLDEN GATE"—REEL.

FRANK LIVINGSTON.

INDY'S FAVORITE—REEL.

THE BLACK-EYED LASSIE—REEL.

HIBERNIA'S PRIDE—REEL.

KILWINNING'S STEEPLE—REEL.

RECREATION—REEL.

MARQUIS OF BOWMONT—REEL.

FLING-DANG—REEL.

NIMBLE FINGER'S—REEL.

LADY BELHAVEN'S—REEL.

SCOTCH

GEN. SHERIDAN'S—REEL.

HARRY CARLETON.

85

STEEPLE CHASE—REEL.

THE RANDY WIFE OF GREENLAW—REEL.

SCOTCH.

PICNIC—REEL.

86

HOWARD—REEL.

D.C.

BECAUSE HE WAS A BONNIE LAD—REEL.
SCOTCH.

"GREAT EASTERN"—REEL.
CLEM. TITUS.

JIMMY HOLMES' FAVORITE—REEL.
SCOTCH.

SMITH'S—REEL.

MERRY NIGHT AT TUMBLE BRIG—REEL.
SCOTCH.

IVY LEAF—REEL.
ZEKE BACKUS.

TOM AND JERRY—REEL.
SCOTCH.

YACHT CLUB—REEL.

LORD JAMES MURRAY'S—REEL.

SCOTCH.

92

7th REGIMENT—REEL.

CONN. HIGGINS.

RATTLE THE BOTTLES—REEL.

SCOTCH.

THE ROCKS OF CASHEL—REEL.

IRISH.

D.C.

"SWALLOW" SLOOP OF WAR—REEL.

MISS DALY'S—REEL.

93

D.C.

DISTANT GREETING—REEL.

B. F. DIETRICH.

NORTH END—REEL.

J. HAND.

FARRELL O'GARA'S FAVORITE—REEL.

D.C.

94

FLETCHER'S DELIGHT—REEL.

D.C.

THE FIRST OF MAY—REEL.

A MINOR.

NEW BEDFORD—REEL.

GREEN GROVES OF ERIN—REEL.

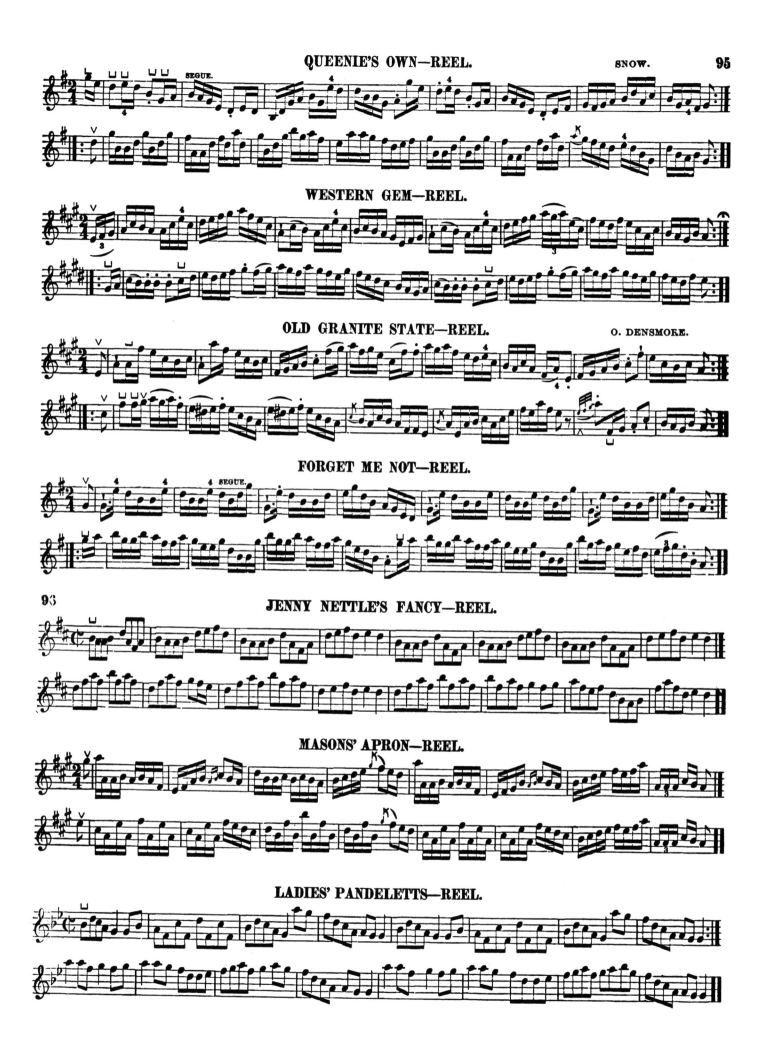

QUEENIE'S OWN—REEL.

WESTERN GEM—REEL.

OLD GRANITE STATE—REEL.

FORGET ME NOT—REEL.

JENNY NETTLE'S FANCY—REEL.

MASONS' APRON—REEL.

LADIES' PANDELETTS—REEL.

PETER STREET—REEL.

THE SAILOR'S RANSOM—REEL.

HOUGH'S FAVORITE—REEL.

THE NORTHERN LIGHT—REEL.

SHAW'S—REEL.

BEN BUTLER'S—REEL.

REPEAL OF THE UNION—REEL.

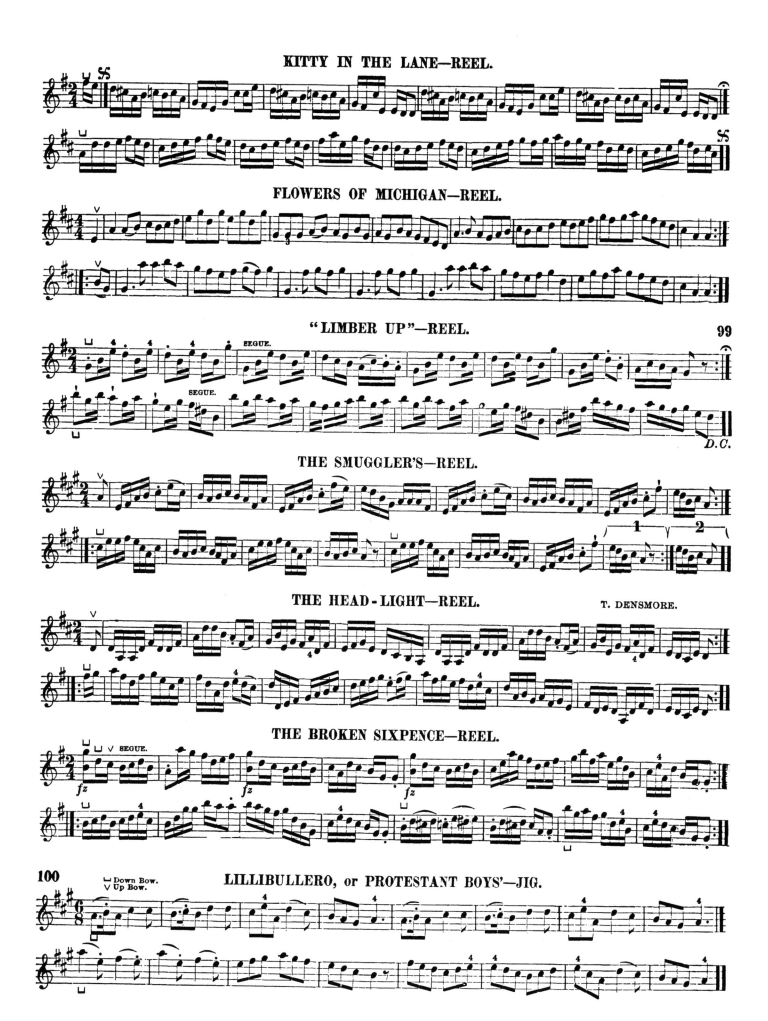

KITTY IN THE LANE—REEL.

FLOWERS OF MICHIGAN—REEL.

"LIMBER UP"—REEL.

99

THE SMUGGLER'S—REEL.

THE HEAD-LIGHT—REEL.

T. DENSMORE.

THE BROKEN SIXPENCE—REEL.

100

⌐ Down Bow.
V Up Bow.

LILLIBULLERO, or PROTESTANT BOYS'—JIG.

MOLL ROE IN THE MORNING—JIG.

HOP—JIG.

LADY CAWDOR'S—JIG.

JOE KENNEDY'S—JIG.

THE BOYS OF BOCKHILL—JIG.

101

TERRY HEIGH—JIG.

BANNOCKS' O' BARLEY MEAL—JIG.

SCOTCH.

LEATHER THE WIG—JIG.

D.S.

POTHOUGE—JIG.

FASTEN THE WIG ON HER—JIG.

THE PRIEST IN HIS BOOTS—JIG.

CATHOLIC BOYS'—JIG.

GO TO THE DEVIL AND SHAKE YOURSELF—JIG.

MORGAN RATTLER—JIG.

COME UNDER MY PLADDIE—JIG.

SIR ROGER DE COVERLY—JIG.

MAGGIE BROWN'S FAVORITE—JIG.

104   LITTLE BROWN JUG—JIG.   JAS. HAND.

MYSTERIES OF KNOCK—JIG.

"PADDY'S THE BOY"—JIG.

HUMOUR OF GLEN—JIG.

MY PRETTY, FAIR MAID—JIG.   105

THE BOTTLE OF BRANDY—JIG.

HASTE TO THE WEDDING—JIG.

TRIP TO GALWAY—JIG.

106

KATY IS WAITING—JIG.

JAS. HAND.

BILLY PATTERSON'S FAVORITE—JIG.

BUNDLE AND GO—JIG.

OLD WALLS OF LISCARROLL—JIG.

D.C.

HAPPY TO MEET, SORRY TO PART—JIG.

107

KATY'S RAMBLES—JIG.

THE COW-BOY'S—JIG.

THE MUNSTER LASS—JIG.

108   COME TO THE RAFFLE—JIG.   JAS. HAND.

HARRINGTON'S HALL—JIG.

IRISHMAN'S HEART TO THE LADIES—JIG.

HARE IN THE CORN—JIG.

THE DRINK OF BRANDY—JIG.

THE GOBBY O—JIG.
(Or JEFFERSON AND LIBERTY.)

PADDY O'RAFFERTY'S—JIG.

D.C.

TELL HER I AM—JIG.

THE WINK OF HER EYE—JIG.

J. HAND.

THE BLOOMING MEADOWS—JIG.

TOP OF CORK ROAD—JIG

OLD MOTHER GOOSE—JIG.

CLOSE TO THE FLOOR—JIG.

J. HAND.   111

FOX HUNTERS'—JIG.

GOLLIHER'S FROLIC—JIG.

EMON ACNUCK—JIG.

112   OFF SHE GOES—JIG.

JACKSON'S MORNING BRUSH—JIG.

D.C.

LITTLE HOUSE UNDER THE HILL—JIG.

THE BRIDAL—JIG.

BARNEY BRALLAGAN'S—JIG.

113

D.C.

THE SOLDIER'S CLOAK—JIG.

CONNAUGHT-MAN'S RAMBLE—JIG.

IRISH WASH-WOMAN—JIG.

114

WHISKEY AND BEER—JIG.

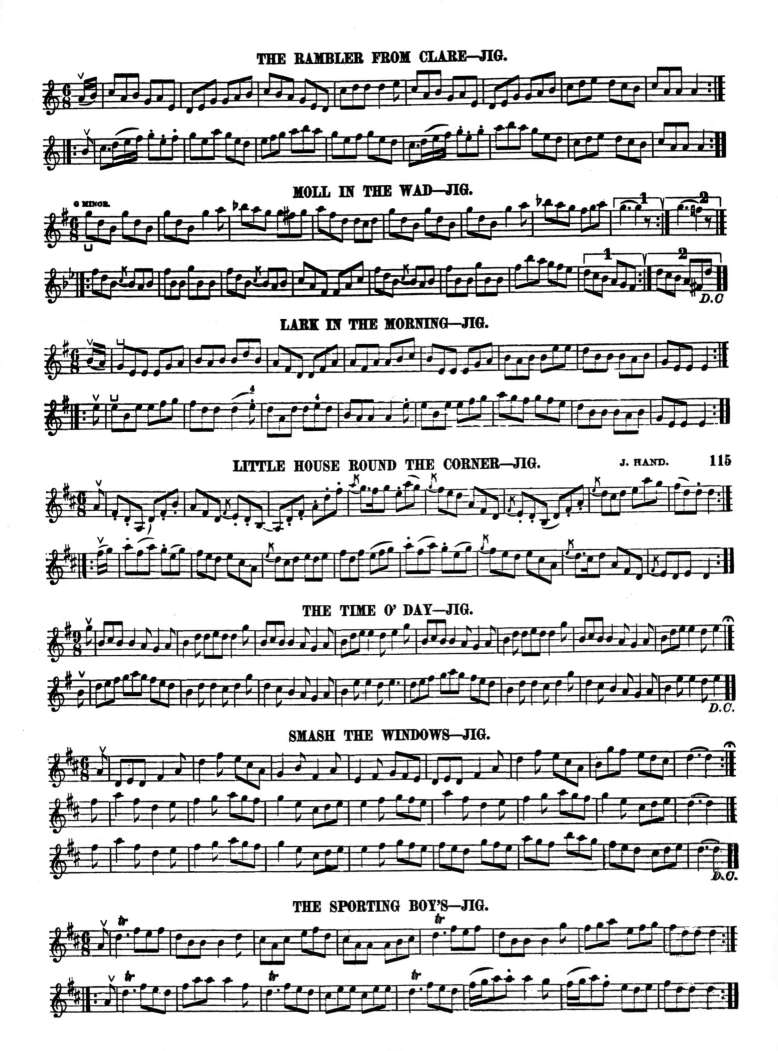

THE RAMBLER FROM CLARE—JIG.

MOLL IN THE WAD—JIG.

LARK IN THE MORNING—JIG.

LITTLE HOUSE ROUND THE CORNER—JIG.

J. HAND.   115

THE TIME O' DAY—JIG.

SMASH THE WINDOWS—JIG.

THE SPORTING BOY'S—JIG.

SAM. HIDE'S—JIG.

RAKES OF KILDARE—JIG

TIVOLI—JIG.

STROP THE RAZOR—JIG.

WIDOW MACHREE—JIG.

LARRY O'GAFF—JIG.

THE UNFORTUNATE RAKE—JIG.

PADDY WHACK—JIG.

THE GREEN FOREVER—JIG.

THE JOYS OF WEDLOCK—JIG.

CATHOLIC BILL'S—JIG.

PRINCE CHARLES'—JIG.

MALONEY'S FANCY—JIG.

D.C.

PADDY WAS UP TO GANGER—JIG.

GOOD MORROW TO YOUR NIGHT-CAP—JIG.

PANDER DANCE—JIG.

120

SUNDAY IS MY WEDDING-DAY—JIG.

SADDLE THE PONY—JIG.

RORY O'MORE—JIG.

OLD FIGARY O'—JIG.

TATTER JACK WELCH—JIG.

121

PANDEEN O'RAFFERTY—JIG.

RIDE A MILE—JIG.

LARRY GROGANS'—JIG.

122   **SPIRITS OF WHISKY—JIG.**

JACKSON'S ROLLING—JIG.

HILLS OF GLENURCHIE—JIG.

SHEE LA NA QUIRA—JIG.

A DROP OF WHISKEY--JIG.

D.C.

PAT IN HIS GLORY--JIG.

LAND OF SWEET ERIN--JIG.

LAND OF SWEET ERIN.—First and 3d couples balance, swing to opposite places—balance there, swing to place; first couple down the centre, back—cast off, right and left.

THE DIAMOND--JIG.

D MINOR.

124

THE WHIM OF A MOMENT--JIG.

R. NAGLE.

KITTY TIRRELL'S--JIG.

THE NIGHT OF FUN--JIG.

JACKSON'S FANCY—JIG.

MRS. HOGAN'S GOOSE—JIG.

J. HAND.

GARRY OWEN—JIG.

GARRY OWEN. (FORE AND AFTER.) *Two couples stand in a line, partners facing each other.* All balance, straight or Highland chain, (this is repeated two or three times) a lady and gent. stop in the centre and balance, straight right and left, other couple the same. Repeat at pleasure.

THE DRUNKEN GANGER'S—JIG.

THE TWO AND SIXPENNY GIRL—JIG.

126

VAUGHAN'S FAVORITE—JIG.

TWO-PENNY POSTMAN'S—JIG.

HIGHWAY TO DUBLIN—JIG.

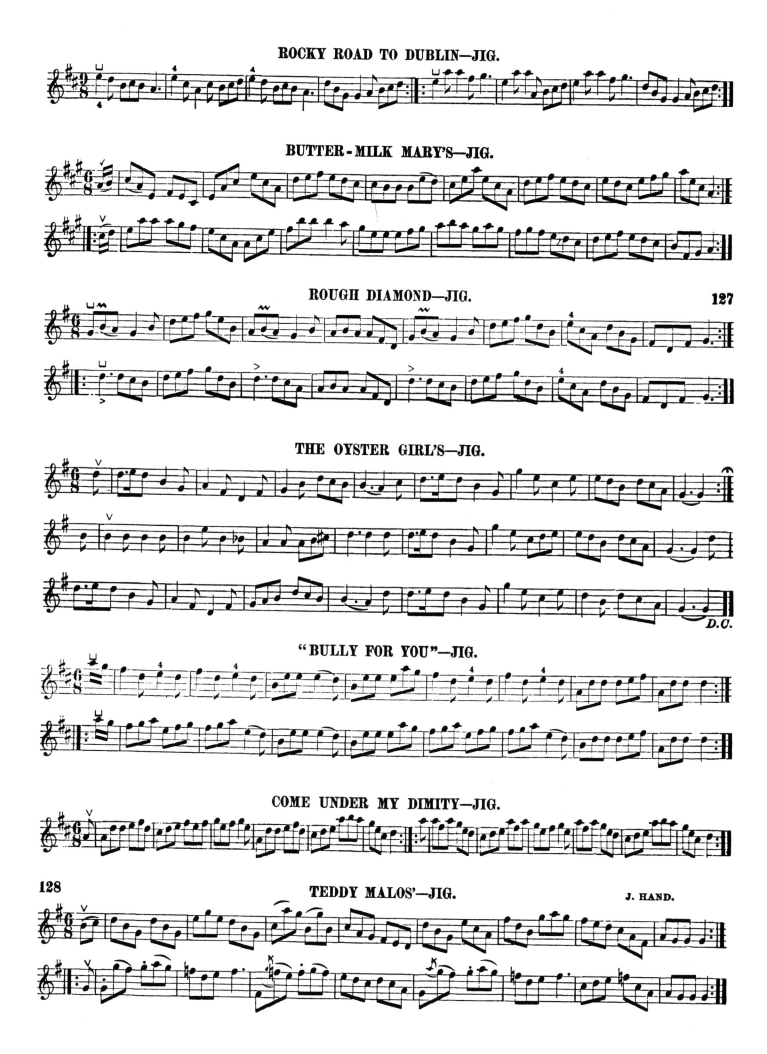

ROCKY ROAD TO DUBLIN—JIG.

BUTTER-MILK MARY'S—JIG.

ROUGH DIAMOND—JIG.

127

THE OYSTER GIRL'S—JIG.

"BULLY FOR YOU"—JIG.

COME UNDER MY DIMITY—JIG.

128

TEDDY MALOS'—JIG.

J. HAND.

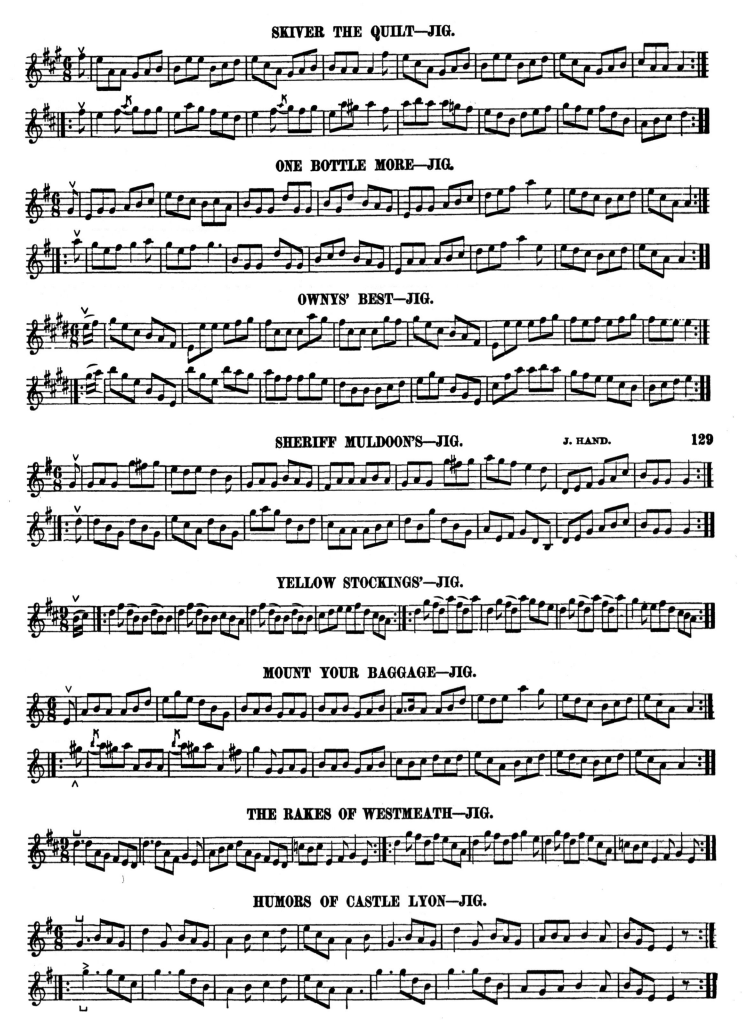

SKIVER THE QUILT—JIG.

ONE BOTTLE MORE—JIG.

OWNYS' BEST—JIG.

SHERIFF MULDOON'S—JIG.   J. HAND.   129

YELLOW STOCKINGS'—JIG.

MOUNT YOUR BAGGAGE—JIG.

THE RAKES OF WESTMEATH—JIG.

HUMORS OF CASTLE LYON—JIG.

KILKENNY ROVER'S—JIG.

LAFRICAN'S—JIG.

THE DUSTY MILLER'S—JIG.

ROSE - BUSH—JIG.

THE COCK AND HEN—JIG.

THE DOUBLE HEAD—JIG.   R. NAGLE.

THREE LITTLE DRUMMERS'—JIG.

THE LIMERICK LASS—JIG.

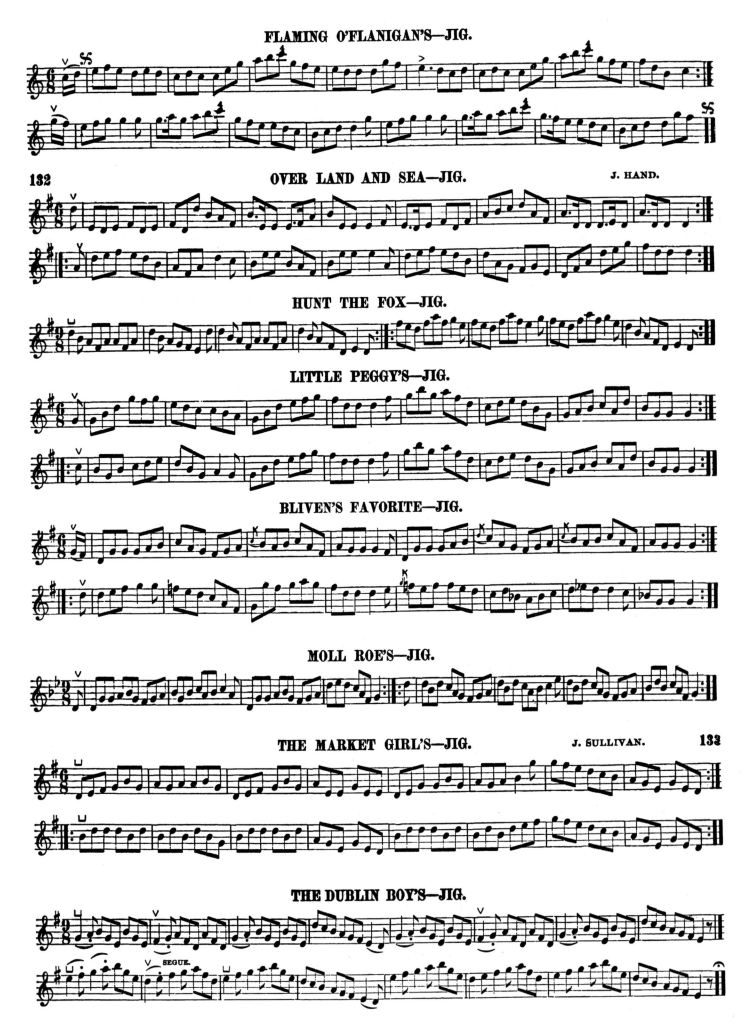

CATCH CLUB—JIG.

PADDY, NOW WONT YOU BE EASY?—JIG.

134 PADDY O'CARROL'S—JIG. J. OSWALD.

O'CONNELL'S WELCOME—JIG.

THE PAUSTEEN FAWN—JIG.

LANIGAN'S BALL—JIG.

NIGHT OF THE FAIR—JIG. H. CAREY. 135

BARNEY'S GOAT—JIG.

SWALLOW-TAIL—JIG.

JOHNNY HAND'S—JIG.

TEETOTAL—JIG.

THE MAID'S COMPLAINT—JIG.

NEAPOLITAN THRESHERS'—JIG.

HEY, CA' THRO'—JIG.

THE BUTCHERS' MARCH—JIG.

100

THE PIVOT BRIG—JIG.

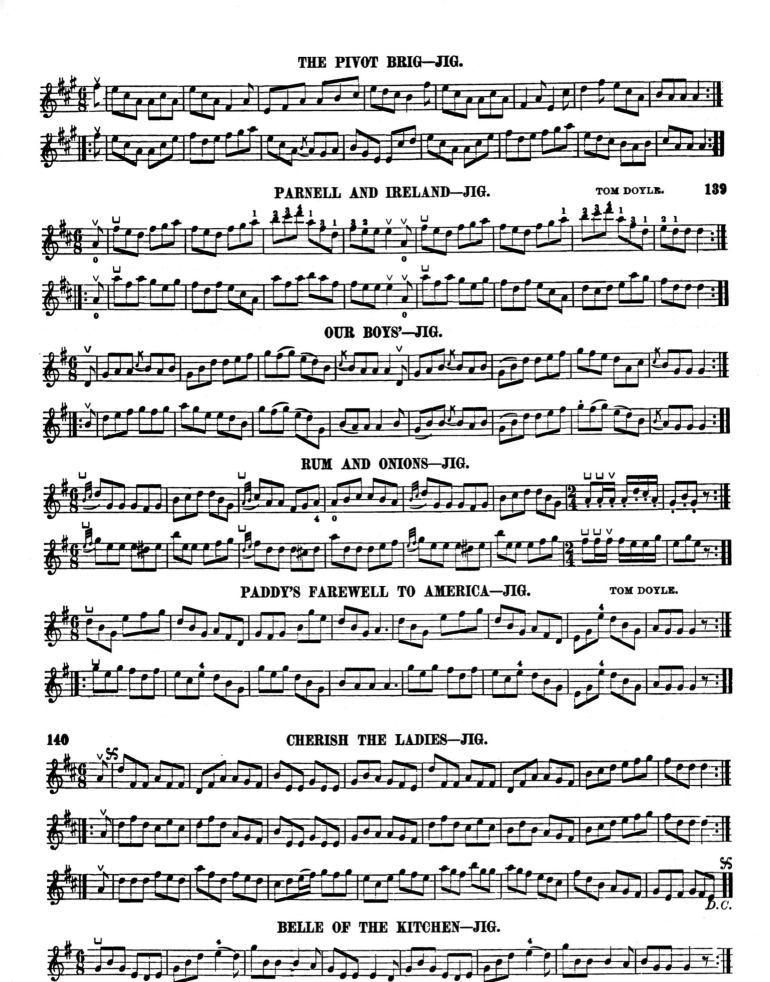

PARNELL AND IRELAND—JIG.

TOM DOYLE.

139

OUR BOYS'—JIG.

RUM AND ONIONS—JIG.

PADDY'S FAREWELL TO AMERICA—JIG.

TOM DOYLE.

140

CHERISH THE LADIES—JIG.

D.C.

BELLE OF THE KITCHEN—JIG.

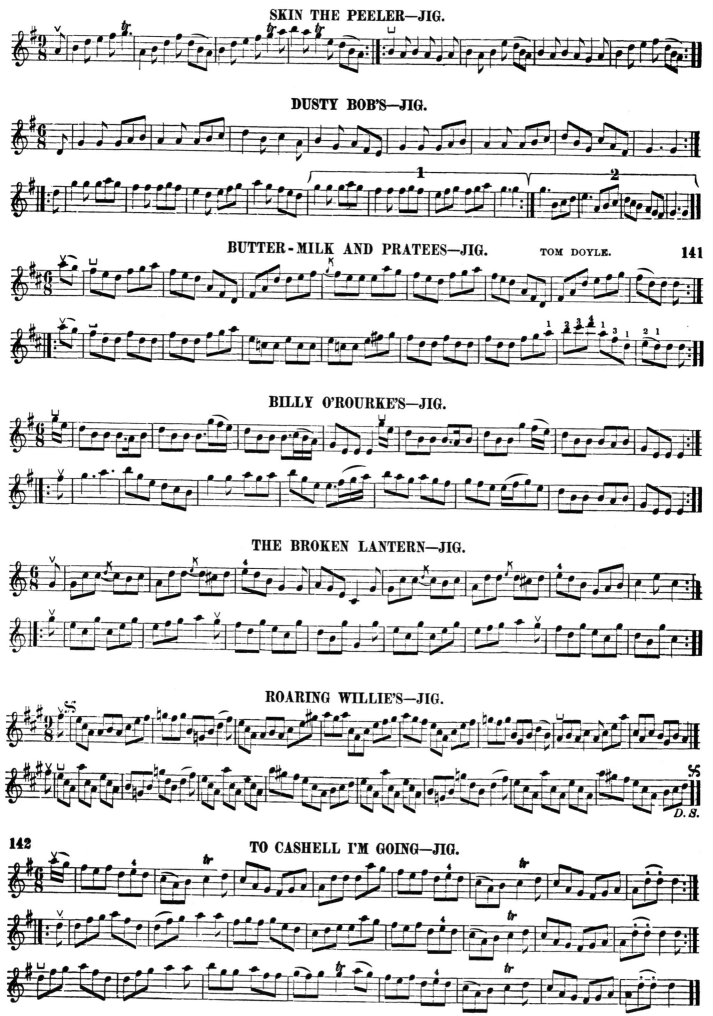

LOVE - LINKS'—JIG.

PUSS IN THE CORNER—JIG.

FAREWELL, SWEET NORA—JIG.

TOM DOYLE.

RUB THE BAG—JIG.

143

THE DEVIL'S OWN SHOT—JIG.

BILLY THE BARBER SHAVED HIS FATHER—JIG.

THE EVICTION—JIG.

THE "LEGACY"—JIG.

SCOTCH.

RIDING ON A HAND-CAR—JIG.

DAYS OF 'LANG SYNE—JIG.

SCOTCH.

THE JOLLY PEDLER'S—JIG.

SLEEPING ON A DOOR-STEP—JIG.

CONN. REGAN.

MAID OF SELMA—JIG.

SCOTCH.

D.S.

KENMURE'S ON AND AWA'—JIG.

SCOTCH.

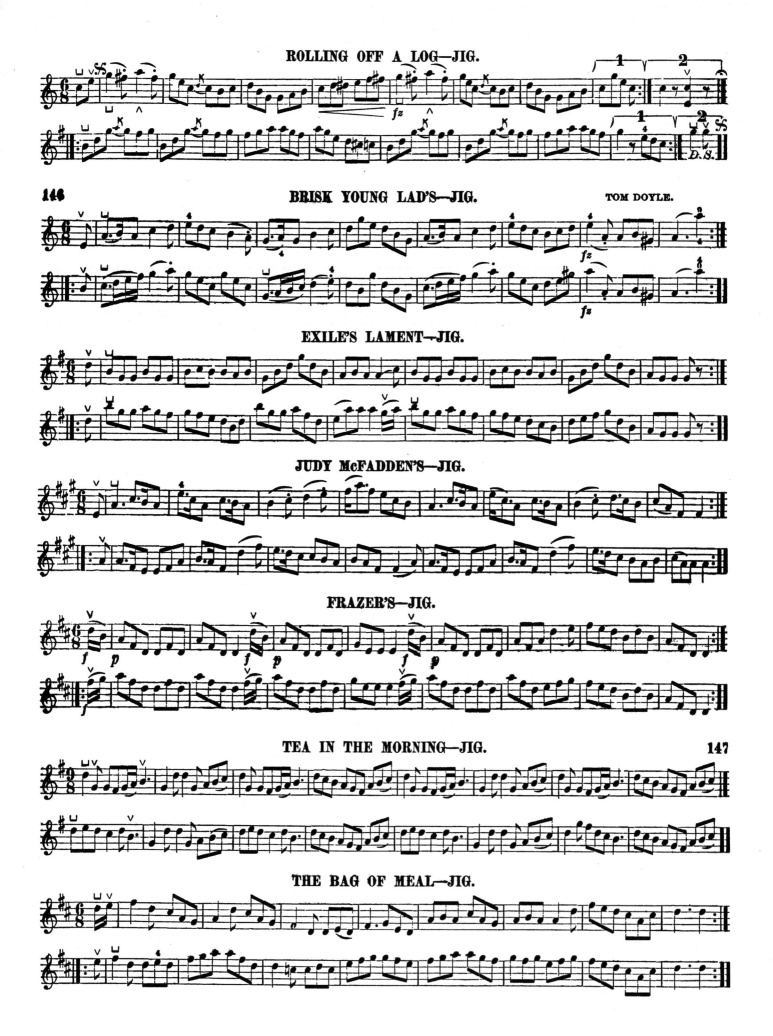

ROLLING OFF A LOG—JIG.

BRISK YOUNG LAD'S—JIG.

TOM DOYLE.

EXILE'S LAMENT—JIG.

JUDY McFADDEN'S—JIG.

FRAZER'S—JIG.

TEA IN THE MORNING—JIG.

THE BAG OF MEAL—JIG.

RED STOCKINGS'—JIG.

SHINS AROUND THE FIRESIDE—JIG.

148

SHUFFLE AND CUT—JIG.
(An Old Irish Dance.)

SWIMMING IN THE GUTTER—JIG.

CONN. REGAN.

LAND LEAGUE—JIG.

TOM DOYLE.

BOBBING FOR EELS—JIG.

O. KNOWLTON.

PADDY CARREY'S FORTUNE—JIG.

149

108

SHORT GRASS—JIG.

CROPPIES, LIE DOWN—JIG.

153

LIMERICK—JIG.

RATTLE THE CASH—JIG.

JACK ON THE GREEN—JIG.

GEESE IN THE BOG—JIG.

154

THE CUSTOM HOUSE—JIG.

TRIP TO THE COTTAGE—JIG.

PRATIES ARE DUG, AND THE FROST IS ALL OVER—JIG.

CONNELLY'S ALE—JIG.

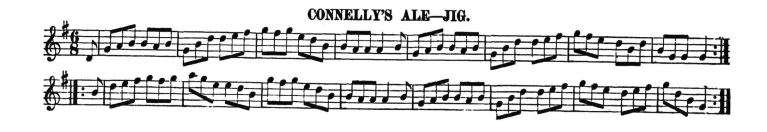

JACKSON'S BOTTLE OF BRANDY—JIG.

155

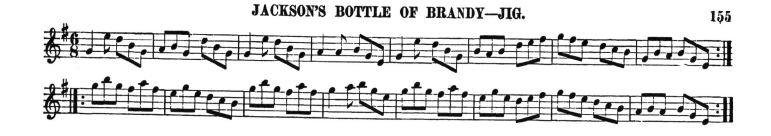

MAID ON THE GREEN—JIG.

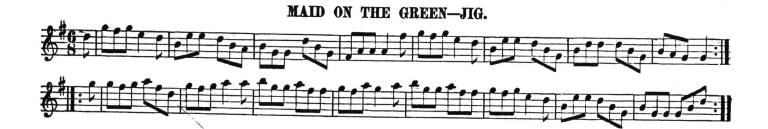

"INDEED! THEN YOU SHANT"—JIG.

MRS. MONROE'S—JIG.

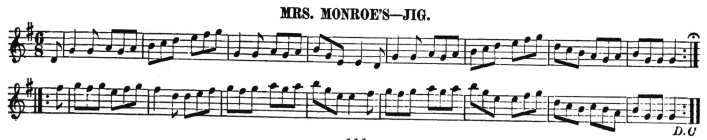

D.C

KITTY O'NEIL'S CHAMPION—JIG.

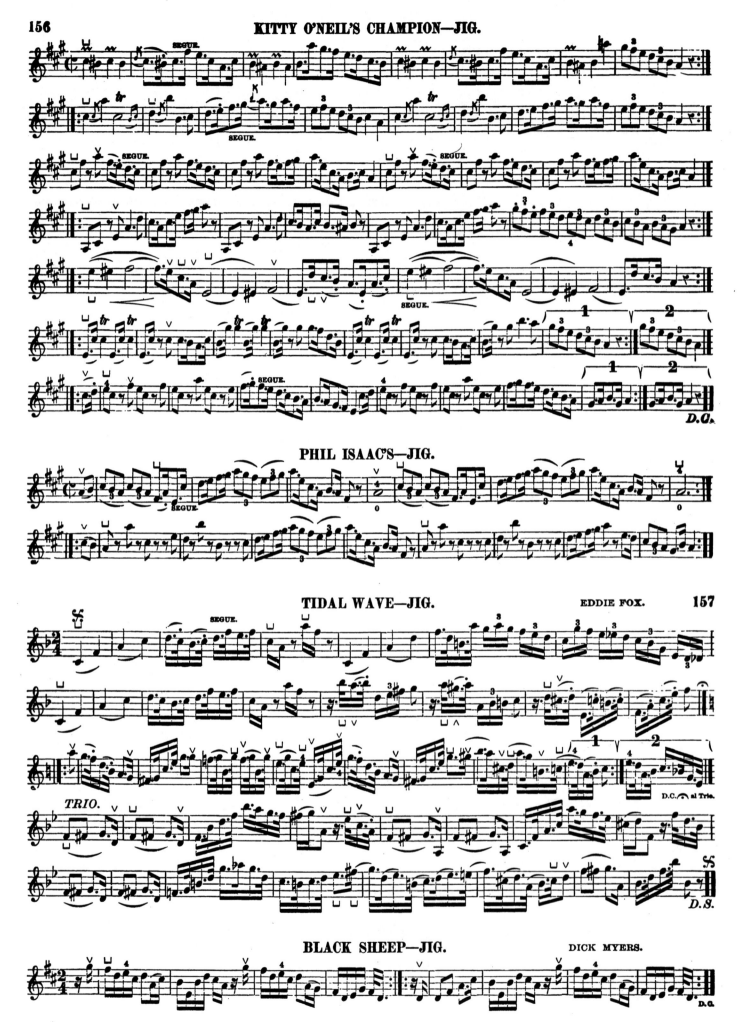

PHIL ISAAC'S—JIG.

TIDAL WAVE—JIG.

EDDIE FOX.

TRIO.

BLACK SHEEP—JIG.

DICK MYERS.

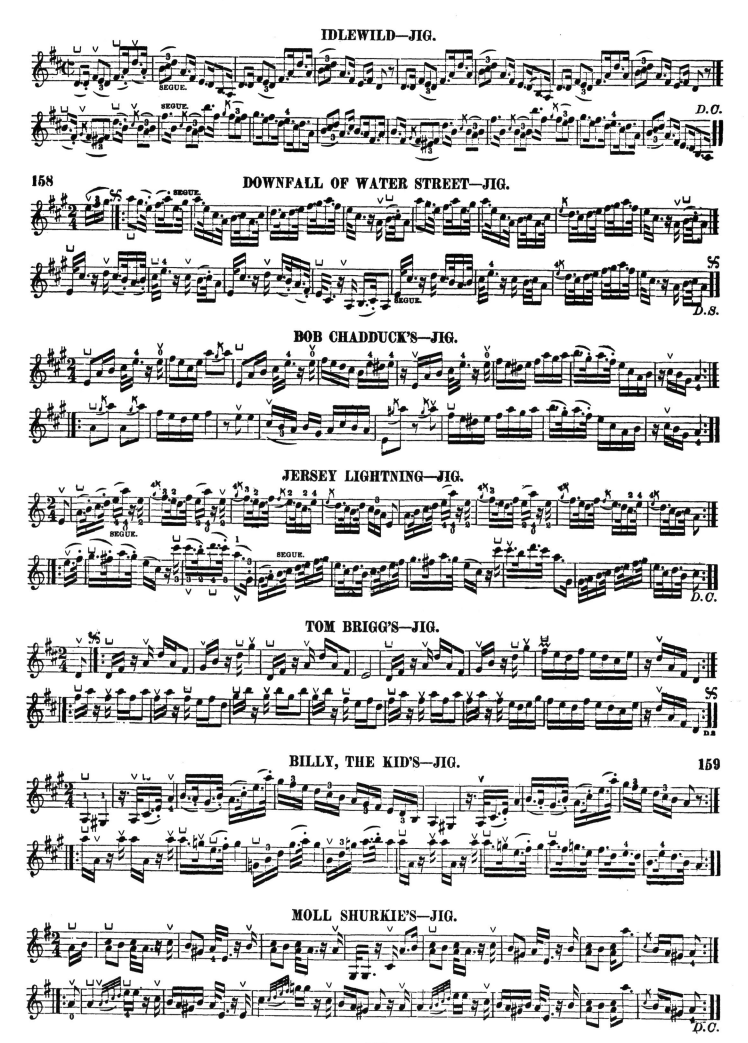

IDLEWILD—JIG.

DOWNFALL OF WATER STREET—JIG.

BOB CHADDUCK'S—JIG.

JERSEY LIGHTNING—JIG.

TOM BRIGG'S—JIG.

BILLY, THE KID'S—JIG.

MOLL SHURKIE'S—JIG.

H—' ON THE WABASH—JIG.

CASTLES IN THE AIR—JIG.

160   CAMP MEETING—JIG.   DAN EMMETT.

NIGGER IN DE WOOD PILE—JIG.

WINNICK'S FAVORITE—JIG.

PEA PATCH—JIG.   DAN EMMETT.

"GET ON DE TRAIN"—JIG.   FRANK LIVINGSTON.   161

114

THE BUTCHER BOY—JIG.

HOLE IN THE WALL—JIG.

162

OAKLAND GARDEN—JIG.

EDWIN CHRISTIE.

LITTLE DIAMOND—JIG.

THE HEADLIGHT—JIG.

HOOP-DE-DOO-DEN-DOO—JIG.

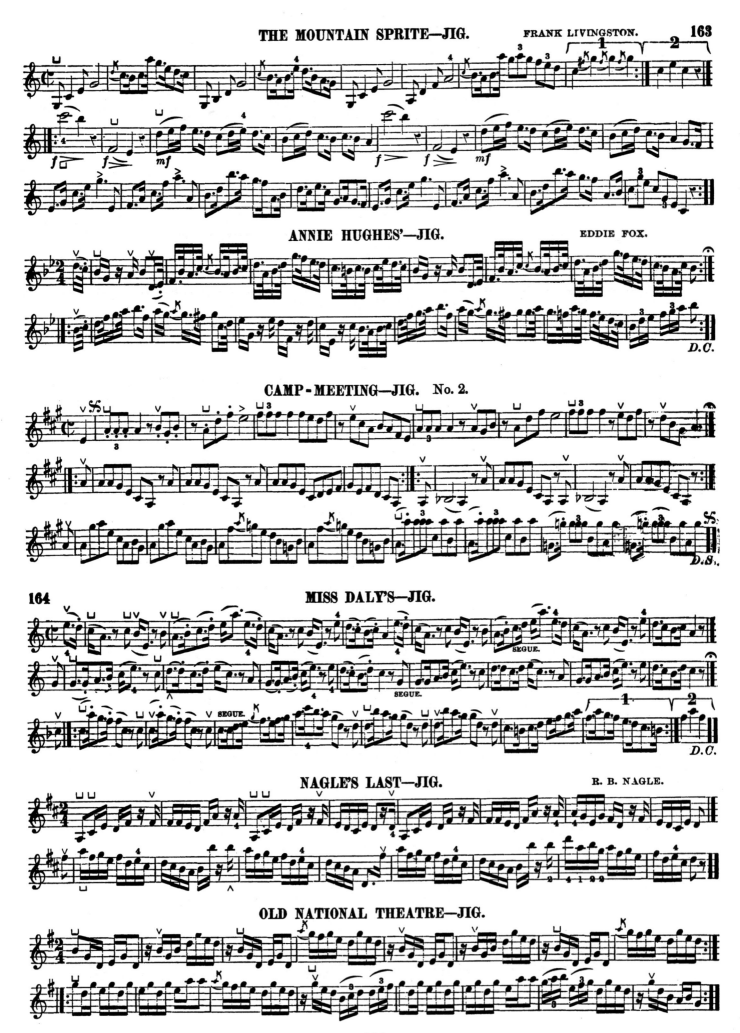

THE MOUNTAIN SPRITE—JIG.

FRANK LIVINGSTON.

ANNIE HUGHES'—JIG.

EDDIE FOX.

CAMP-MEETING—JIG. No. 2.

MISS DALY'S—JIG.

NAGLE'S LAST—JIG.

R. B. NAGLE.

OLD NATIONAL THEATRE—JIG.

JAMES LEE'S FAVORITE—JIG.

D.S.

ROOT, HOG, OR DIE—JIG.

HARRY BLOODGOOD'S FAMOUS—JIG.

167

DAR'S SUGAR IN DE GOURD—JIG.

JAMES BUCKLEY.

WILLIAMS AND SULLIVAN'S—JIG.

HANG FIRE—JIG.

168

Down Bow.
Up Bow.

NORFOLK—HORNPIPE.

W. H. WHIDDON.

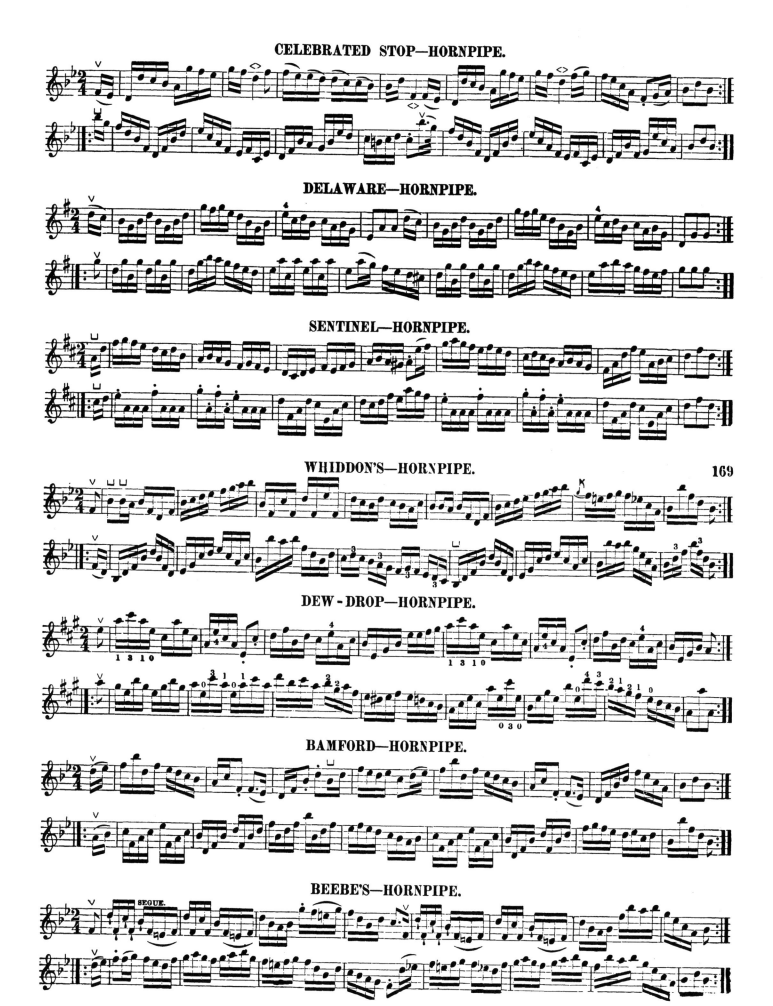

CELEBRATED STOP—HORNPIPE.

DELAWARE—HORNPIPE.

SENTINEL—HORNPIPE.

WHIDDON'S—HORNPIPE.

169

DEW - DROP—HORNPIPE.

BAMFORD—HORNPIPE.

BEEBE'S—HORNPIPE.

ALDRIDGE'S—HORNPIPE.

PORTSMOUTH—HORNPIPE.

SEBASTAPOL—HORNPIPE.

SCOTCH—HORNPIPE.

SALEM—HORNPIPE.

P. S. GILMORE.

COLLEGE—HORNPIPE.

COLLEGE HORNPIPE.—First lady balance to 3d gent, turn 2d gent; 1st gent. balance to 3d lady, turn with 3d lady; 1st couple down the centre, back, cast off, right and left.

BLANCHARD'S—HORNPIPE.

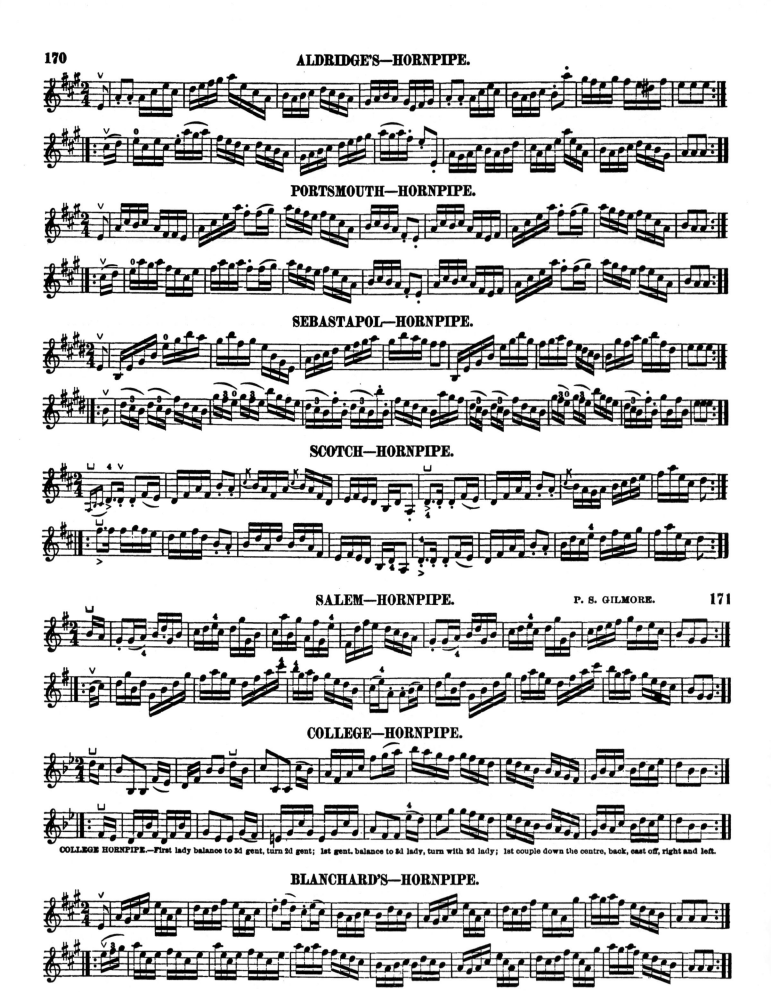

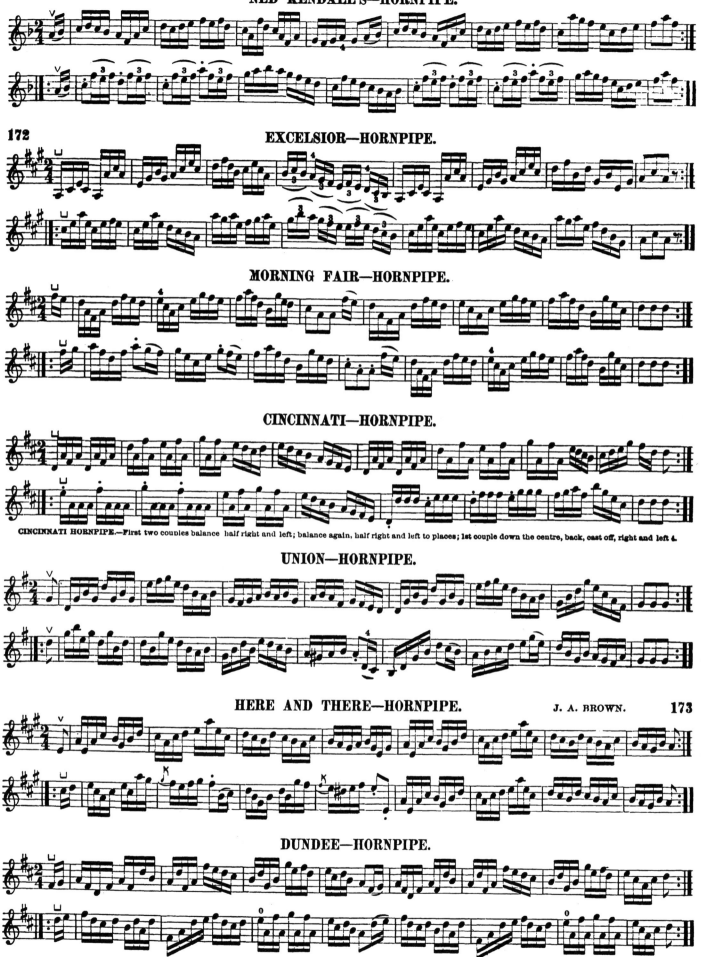

NED KENDALL'S—HORNPIPE.

172 EXCELSIOR—HORNPIPE.

MORNING FAIR—HORNPIPE.

CINCINNATI—HORNPIPE.

CINCINNATI HORNPIPE.—First two couples balance half right and left; balance again, half right and left to places; 1st couple down the centre, back, cast off, right and left 4.

UNION—HORNPIPE.

HERE AND THERE—HORNPIPE.   J. A. BROWN.   **173**

DUNDEE—HORNPIPE.

CORINTHIAN—HORNPIPE.

CORINTHIAN HORNPIPE.—First couple down the centre with 2d lady, (leave lady at the foot), back; first couple down the centre with 2d gent. (leave 2d gent. at the foot), back; first couple down the outside, pass in to centre at the foot; up the centre, followed by 2d couple; right and left.

HAND ORGAN—HORNPIPE.

HAND-ORGAN HORNPIPE.—First couple cross over, and go between 2d and 3d couples, facing out; join hands and balance three on a side, and swing the right hand person; balance again, swing the left hand person, and partners half round with right hand; first couple down the centre, back; cast off, right and left.

174

LONDON—HORNPIPE.

PARRY'S—HORNPIPE.

RED LION—HORNPIPE.

RED LION HORNPIPE.—First couple balance, down centre; balance at foot, up the centre and cast off; cross right hands half round, left hands back; right and left 4.

PUSHEE'S—HORNPIPE.

A. PUSHEE.

GOLDEN EAGLE—HORNPIPE.

175

THE FORESTER'S—HORNPIPE.

LIVERPOOL—HORNPIPE.

FIJIYAMA—HORNPIPE.
(Can be used as a Clog.)

176

AMATEUR—HORNPIPE.
(Can be used as a Clog.)

J. HAND.

HIGHLAND—HORNPIPE.

NEW CENTURY—HORNPIPE.

NEW CENTURY HORNPIPE.—First couple balance, swing once and a half round; ladies' chain; First couple balance again, swing once and a half round to place; right and left 4.

GLOBE—HORNPIPE.

DE GOLYER—HORNPIPE.

GARFIELD.

ALBEMARLE—HORNPIPE.

RICKETT'S—HORNPIPE.

RICKETT'S HORNPIPE.—First 6 balance, swing half round, balance again, swing to places.   First couple down the centre, back;   cast off—right and left.

GLOBE - TROTTER—HORNPIPE.

(*Can be used as a Clog.*)

HIAWATHA—HORNPIPE.

ARIEL—HORNPIPE.

VINTON'S—HORNPIPE.

VINTON'S HORNPIPE.—First lady balance to 1st and 2d gents, three hands round; first gent. balance to 1st and 2d ladies, three hands round.—First couple down the centre, back and cast off: right and left.

BIRMINGHAM—HORNPIPE.

BROOKSIDE—HORNPIPE.

WILLOTT'S—HORNPIPE.

DEMOCRATIC—HORNPIPE.

BALKAN—HORNPIPE.

HAYES.

JIMMY LINN'S—HORNPIPE.

(Can be used as a Clog.)

J. L.

JINRIKISHA—HORNPIPE.

SMITH'S—HORNPIPE.

SMITH'S HORNPIPE.—First and 2d couples cross right hands half round.—First couple down the centre, back; first and 2d couples cross left hands half round to place. First couple down the centre, back, cast off; right and left.

PRINCE ALBERT'S—HORNPIPE.

BEES' WINGS—HORNPIPE.
(Can be used as a Clog.)

181

BRICK - LAYERS'—HORNPIPE.

BRICK-LAYERS' HORNPIPE.—First couple cross over (inside) below 2d couple, up on the outside, swing partner to place. First couple down the centre, back; cast off—First lady swing 2d gent. quite round; first gent swing 2d lady quite round; right and left.

JIM CLARK'S—HORNPIPE.

EVERY- BODY'S—HORNPIPE.
(Can be used as a Clog.

182

COSMOPOLITAN—HORNPIPE.
(Can be used as a Clog.)

As performed by J. HAND

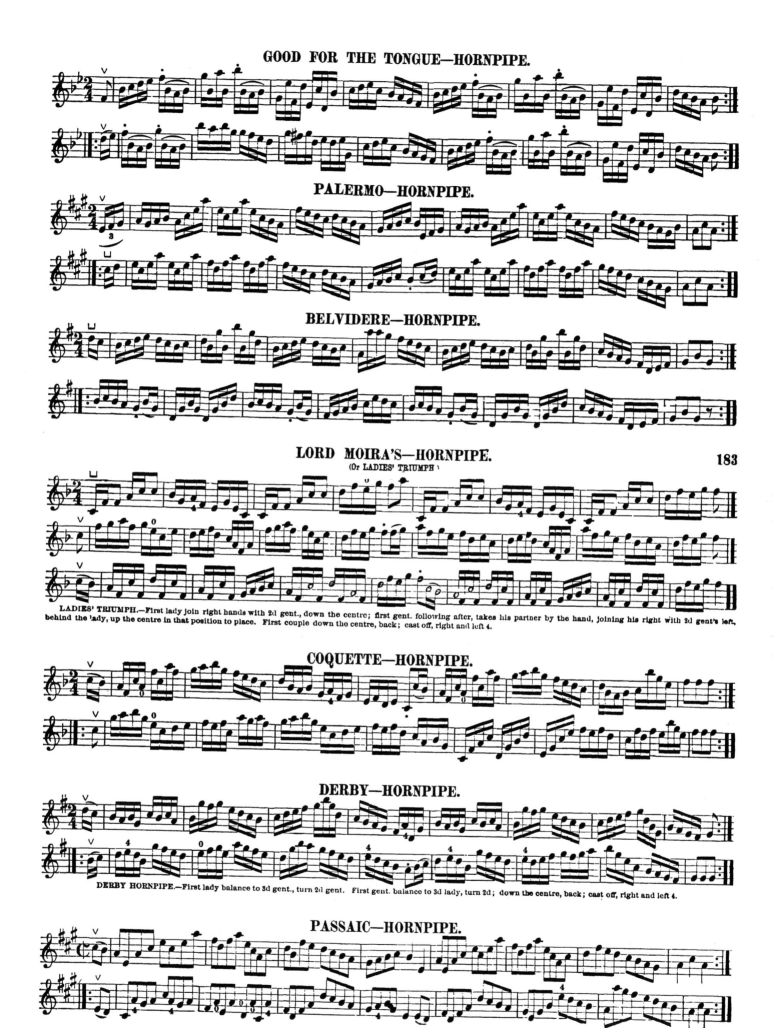

GOOD FOR THE TONGUE—HORNPIPE.

PALERMO—HORNPIPE.

BELVIDERE—HORNPIPE.

LORD MOIRA'S—HORNPIPE.
(Or LADIES' TRIUMPH)

LADIES' TRIUMPH.—First lady join right hands with 2d gent., down the centre; first gent. following after, takes his partner by the hand, joining his right with 2d gent's left, behind the lady, up the centre in that position to place. First couple down the centre, back; cast off, right and left 4.

COQUETTE—HORNPIPE.

DERBY—HORNPIPE.

DERBY HORNPIPE.—First lady balance to 3d gent., turn 2d gent. First gent. balance to 3d lady, turn 2d; down the centre, back; cast off, right and left 4.

PASSAIC—HORNPIPE.

CHAMPION—HORNPIPE.
(Can be used as a clog.)

As performed by J. HAND.

DURANG'S—HORNPIPE.

DURANG'S HORNPIPE.—First couple balance, cross over below two couples, balance there, cross back to places; down the centre, back; cast off, right and left.

ORIENTAL—HORNPIPE.

CUPIDO—HORNPIPE.

VICTORIA—HORNPIPE.
(Can be used as a Clog.)

As performed by J. HAND

MASSASOIT—HORNPIPE.

LAMP-LIGHTERS'—HORNPIPE.

LAMP-LIGHTERS' HORNPIPE.—First couple cross over and go between 2d and 3d couples, facing out; join hands and balance, three on a side, and swing the right hand person; balance again, swing the left hand person, and swing partners half round with right hand; First couple down the centre, back, cast off, right and left.

LOCKER'S—HORNPIPE.

186 DEFIANCE—HORNPIPE.

As performed by R. TISON

EUREKA—HORNPIPE.

WHIPPLE'S—HORNPIPE.

WHIPPLE'S HORNPIPE.—First couple down the centre, turn half round; back, (lady on gent's side, gent. on ladies' side), cast off, ladies' chain. half promenade, half right and left to places.

TRAFALGAR—HORNPIPE.

SANS SOUCI—HORNPIPE.   G. L. TRACY.   **187**

PALMETTO—HORNPIPE.

FISHER'S—HORNPIPE.

FISHER'S HORNPIPE.—First couple down the outside, back; down the centre, back; cast off; swing 6 hands quite round; right and left.

MARSHALL HILL'S—HORNPIPE.

188

COPENHAGEN—HORNPIPE.
(Can be used as a Clog.)

IDYL—HORNPIPE.
(Can be used as a Clog.)

CROTON—HORNPIPE.

MINEAPOLIS—HORNPIPE.
(Can be used as a Clog.)

FERRY BRIDGE—HORNPIPE.
(Can be used as a Clog.)

As performed by J. HAND.

189

SUMNER'S—HORNPIPE.

PRINCESS—HORNPIPE.
(Can be used as a Clog.)

RANDALL'S—HORNPIPE.

190   ELECTRIC—HORNPIPE.
G. L. TRACY.

ASPINWALL—HORNPIPE.

NORTH STAR—HORNPIPE.

JAUNTING - CAR—HORNPIPE.
J. HAND.
(Can be used as a Clog.)

NYMROD—HORNPIPE.
(Can be used as a Clog.)

G. L. TRACY.

BONANZA—HORNPIPE

POPPY LEAF—HORNPIPE.
(Can be used as a Clog.)

THUNDER—HORNPIPE.

THUNDER HORNPIPE.—First lady balance to 2d and 3d gents., 3 hands round; first gent. balance to 1st and 2d ladies, 3 hands round; first couple down the centre, back, cast off—right and left.

LINCOLN'S—HORNPIPE.
(Can be used as a Clog.)

TEXARKANA—HORNPIPE.

ST. ELMO—HORNPIPE.

BALL AND PIN—HORNPIPE.

ACROBAT'S—HORNPIPE.
(Can be used as a Clog.)

As performed by G. L. TRACY.

193

STATEN ISLAND—HORNPIPE.

AMAZON—HORNPIPE.
(Can be used as a Clog.)

KEY-WEST—HORNPIPE.

194

NATIONAL GUARDS'—HORNPIPE.
(Can be used as a Clog.)

As performed by J. HAND.

YPSILANTI—HORNPIPE.

SPIRIT OF 1881—HORNPIPE.

AUTOGRAPH—HORNPIPE.
(Can be used as a Clog.)

RIALTO—HORNPIPE.
(Can be used as a Clog.)

As performed by G. L. TRACY.

195

MISS BARKER'S—HORNPIPE.

VIOLETTA—HORNPIPE.

FLOCKTON'S—HORNPIPE.

SEGUE.

SEGUE.

196

GO AS YOU PLEASE—HORNPIPE.
(Can be used as a Clog.)

As performed by G. L. TRACY.

DICK SAND'S—HORNPIPE.
(Can be used as a Clog.)

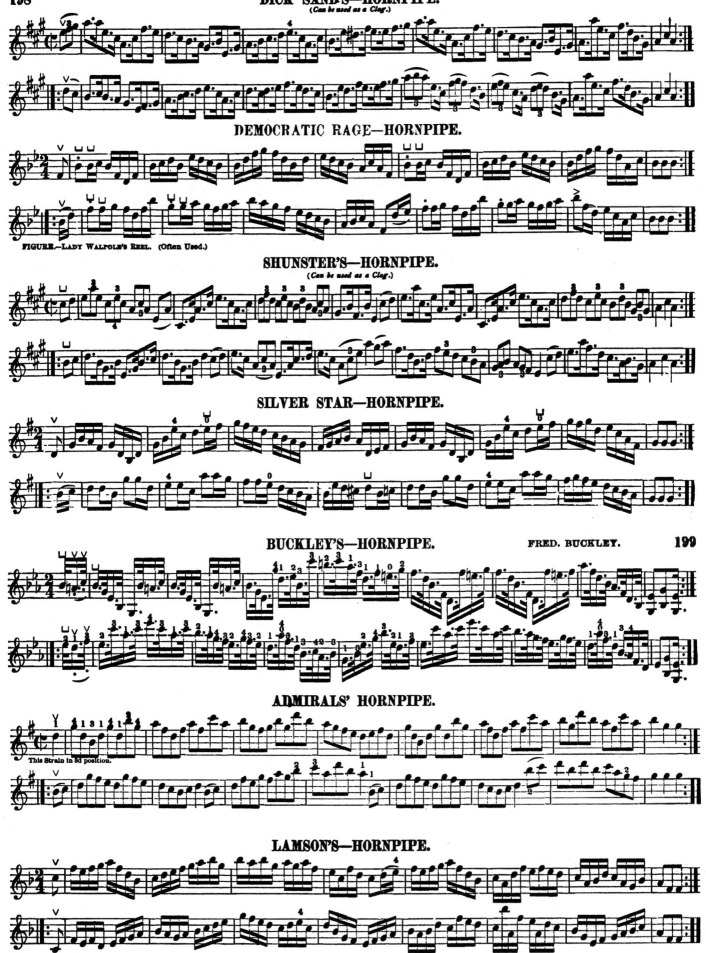

DEMOCRATIC RAGE—HORNPIPE.

FIGURE.—LADY WALPOLE'S REEL. (Often Used.)

SHUNSTER'S—HORNPIPE.
(Can be used as a Clog.)

SILVER STAR—HORNPIPE.

BUCKLEY'S—HORNPIPE.
FRED. BUCKLEY.

ADMIRALS' HORNPIPE.

This Strain in 3d position.

LAMSON'S—HORNPIPE.

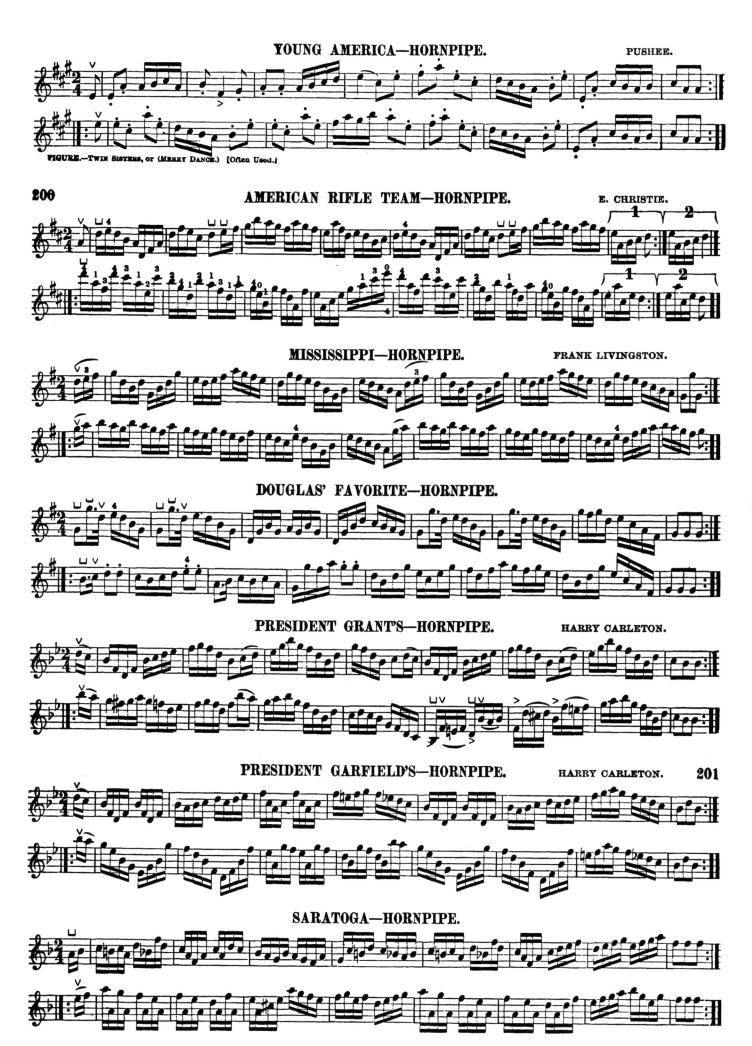

YOUNG AMERICA—HORNPIPE.

PUSHEE.

FIGURE.—TWIN SISTERS, or (MERRY DANCE.) [Often Used.]

200

AMERICAN RIFLE TEAM—HORNPIPE.

E. CHRISTIE.

MISSISSIPPI—HORNPIPE.

FRANK LIVINGSTON.

DOUGLAS' FAVORITE—HORNPIPE.

PRESIDENT GRANT'S—HORNPIPE.

HARRY CARLETON.

PRESIDENT GARFIELD'S—HORNPIPE.

HARRY CARLETON.

201

SARATOGA—HORNPIPE.

WADE HAMPTON'S—HORNPIPE.

FRANK LIVINSTON.

QUEEN OF THE WEST—HORNPIPE.

ZEKE BACKUS.

MOUNTAIN RANGER—HORNPIPE.

202

MOUNTAIN RANGER. (First couple cross over.) First lady down the centre with 2d gent, and back. (Same time.) First gent balance with 2d lady, and turn. First gent down the centre with 2d lady, and back. (Same time.) First lady balance to 2d gent, and turn. First couple down the centre and back, cast off. Ladies' chain.

ELKS' FESTIVAL—HORNPIPE.
(Can be used as a Clog.)

HUNTSMANS'—HORNPIPE.

OCCIDENTAL—HORNPIPE.

NIAGARA—HORNPIPE.

203

NIAGARA HORNPIPE.—First couple down the outside, back and cross over: First lady balance with 2d gent, (Same time first gent. balance with 2d lady.) First couple swing to place, ladies' chain. Right and left 4.

138

QUINDARO HORNPIPE.—First and 3d couples balance, swing 6 hands half round; balance again, swing 6 hands round to place; First couple down the centre; back, cast off, righl and left 4.

CURT LAWRENCE'S—HORNPIPE.

FAVORITE—HORNPIPE.

HULL'S VICTORY—HORNPIPE.

HULL'S VICTORY. First couple give right hands and swing half round, (First lady give left hand to 2d gent's right, gent. give left hand to 2d lady's right,) balance 4 in a line; First lady swing with 2d gent, first gent. swing with 2d lady at same time and pass partner; join hands again with 2d couple, balance 4 in a line, swing to places, down the centre with partner, up, cast off, right and left 4.

COLBERTH'S—HORNPIPE.

"GEORGIA CRACKERS"—HORNPIPE.

FRANK LIVINGSTON.

TIN WEDDING—HORNPIPE.

TELEGRAPH—HORNPIPE.

HALL.

NEWS BOYS'—HORNPIPE.

NATIONAL LANCERS'—HORNPIPE.

HARRY CARLETON.

207

MAZEPPA—HORNPIPE.
(Can be used as a Clog.)

ERIE—HORNPIPE.

ST. PIERRE—HORNPIPE.

208

HUMOURS OF BOSTON—HORNPIPE.

FANTASTIC—HORNPIPE.
(Can be used as a Clog.)

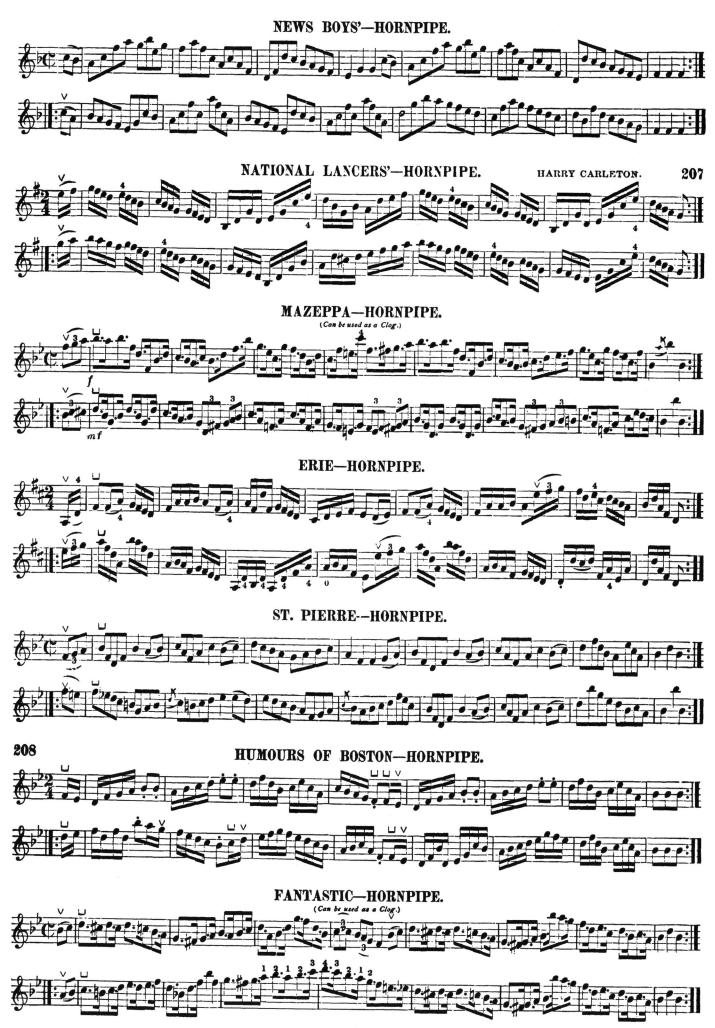

TETE - A - TETE—HORNPIPE.   HARRY CARLETON.

BELLE OF CLAREMONT—HORNPIPE.

CITY OF SAVANNAH—HORNPIPE.   FRANK LIVINGSTON   209

OYSTER RIVER—HORNPIPE.

OYSTER RIVER.—First couple balance to 2d gent, 3 hands round; First couple balance to 2d lady, 3 hands round; First couple down the centre, back; cast off; Right and left 4.

OLYMPIC—HORNPIPE.
(Can be used as a Clog.)

NELSON'S VICTORY—HORNPIPE.

210   "TERPSICHOREAN"—HORNPIPE.

MISS MOUNTAN'S—HORNPIPE.

CHASE THE SQUIRREL—First lady down the outside, (gent crosses over and follows,) back, up the centre of set; First gent down the outside, (lady crosses over and follows,) back, up the centre; First couple join hands, down the centre and back; cast off, right and left 4.

NORTON'S FAVORITE—HORNPIPE.
(Can be used as a Clog.)

CUCKOO—HORNPIPE.

GOLDEN WEDDING—HORNPIPE.

211

RED CROSS—HORNPIPE.

NATIONAL—HORNPIPE.

BELLE OF THE BALL—HORNPIPE.

BELLE OF THE BALL.—First couple down the outside, back; down the centre, back; cast off, chassa across with the 2d couple, back, right and left with 2d couple.

MAID IN THE PUMP-ROOM—HORNPIPE.

MAID IN THE PUMP-ROOM.—First lady down the centre, (first gent down the outside at same time,) back; First gent down the centre, (First lady down the outside at same time,) back; First couple down the the centre, back; cast off, right and left 4.

CAMP MEETING—HORNPIPE.

HARRY CARLETON.

JOCK TAMSON'S—HORNPIPE.

"CUPID'S FROLIC"—HORNPIPE.

"BEAUTIFUL SWANEE RIVER"—HORNPIPE.

HARRY CARLETON. 213

DEER-FOOT—HORNPIPE.

COLUMBIA—HORNPIPE.

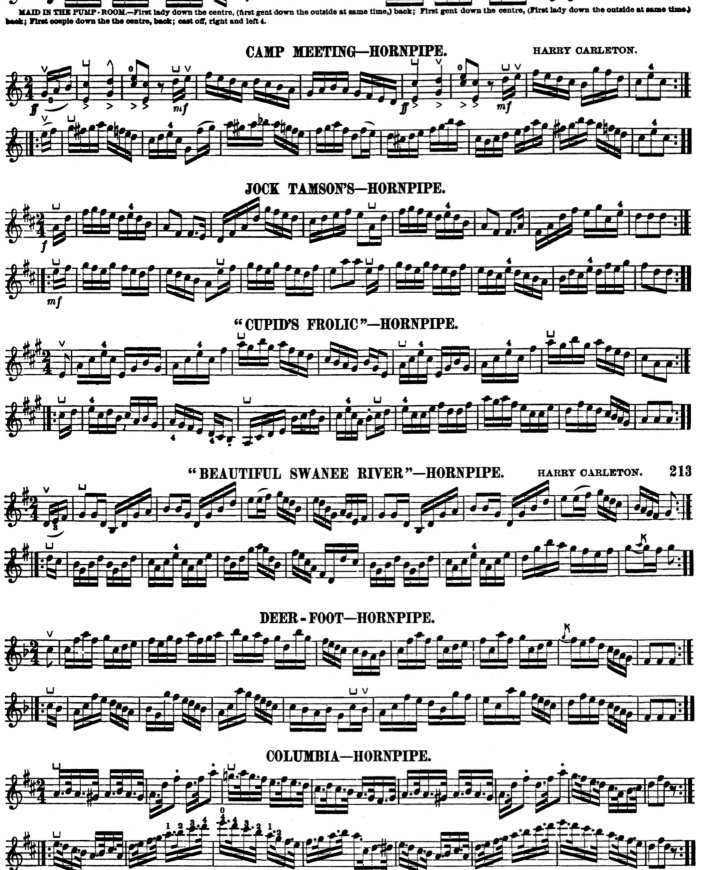

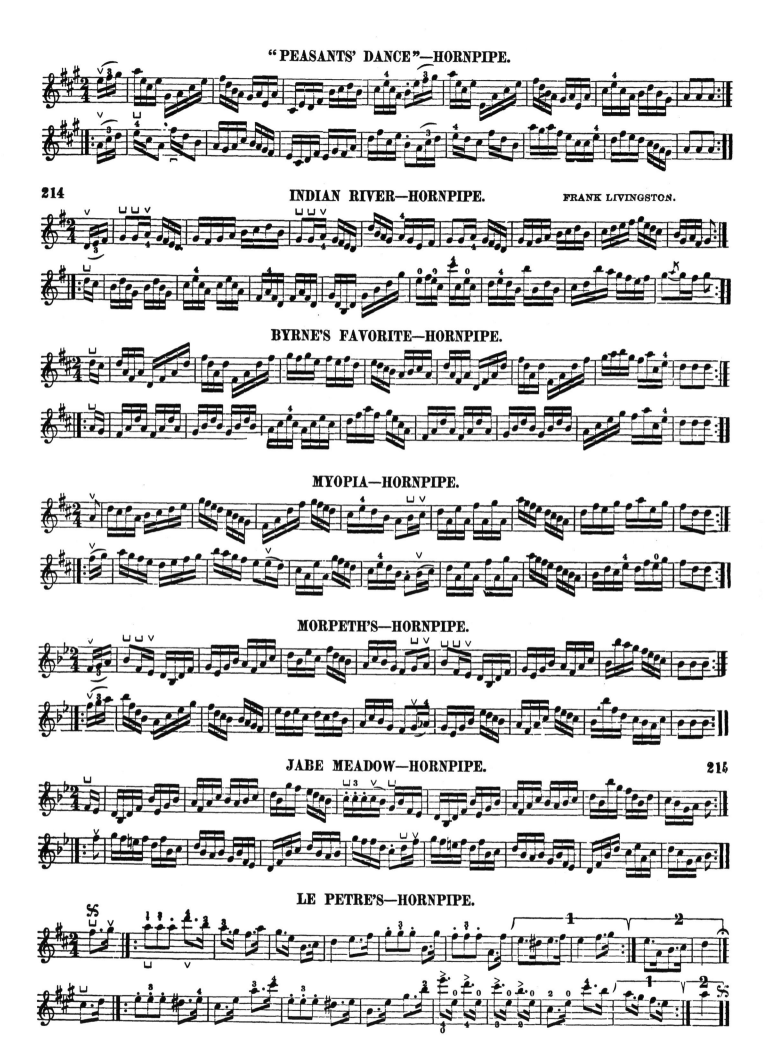

"PEASANTS' DANCE"—HORNPIPE.

INDIAN RIVER—HORNPIPE.   FRANK LIVINGSTON.

BYRNE'S FAVORITE—HORNPIPE.

MYOPIA—HORNPIPE.

MORPETH'S—HORNPIPE.

JABE MEADOW—HORNPIPE.

LE PETRE'S—HORNPIPE.

MONOGRAM—HORNPIPE.

ATLANTA—HORNPIPE.

216
DUXBURY—HORNPIPE.
N. SAMPSON.

PARASOTT—HORNPIPE.

GOLDEN WREATH—HORNPIPE.

CALISTHENIC—HORNPIPE.

SOUVENIR DE VENICE—HORNPIPE.

L. OSTINELLI.

BEST SHOT—HORNPIPE.
(Can be used as a Clog.)

APOLLO CLUB—HORNPIPE.

PRIMA DONNA—HORNPIPE.

DANISH—HORNPIPE.

VELOCIPEDE—HORNPIPE.
(Can be used as a Clog.)

STEAMBOAT HORNPIPE.

FLORIDA CRACKERS'—HORNPIPE.

FRANK LIVINGSTON.   219

MAID MARIAN—HORNPIPE.

RICKER'S—HORNPIPE.

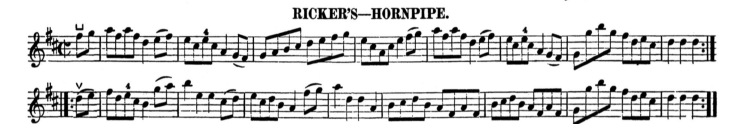

VESTRI'S—HORNPIPE.
(Can be used as a Clog.)

220   ## VENDOME—HORNPIPE.
(Can be used as a Clog.)

BUENA VISTA—HORNPIPE.

BUENA VISTA.—First couple cross over, balance between 2d and 3d couples, (joining hands and facing out,) turn with right hands; balance again, (in same position) turn with left hands; (lady remains on gents side, gent on lady's side,) down the centre, back; cast off; ladies' chain.

ST CLAIR'S—HORNPIPE.

PEERLESS HORNPIPE.

CASTLE—HORNPIPE.

KING COLBATH.

221

BURNS' IRISH—HORNPIPE.

JACK'S ALIVE—HORNPIPE.

CARNIVAL—HORNPIPE.
(Can be used as a Clog.)

222

CHANDLER'S HORNPIPE.

LEVIATHAN—HORNPIPE.

ALMACK'S—HORNPIPE.
(Can be used as a Ciog.)

TELEPHONE—HORNPIPE.

BELLES OF SOUTH BOSTON—HORNPIPE.

223

MADAME DEL CARO'S—HORNPIPE.

HUMPHREY'S—HORNPIPE.

CALIFORNIA—HORNPIPE.

CZAR OF RUSSIA'S FAVORITE—HORNPIPE.

D.C.

OBELISK—HORNPIPE.

MISS JESS. WATSON'S—HORNPIPE.

"SALLY GROWLER"—HORNPIPE.

HARRY CARLETON.

BABBIT'S—HORNPIPE.

STAR OF THE EAST—HORNPIPE.

(Can be used as a Clog.)

PASSION - FLOWER—HORNPIPE.

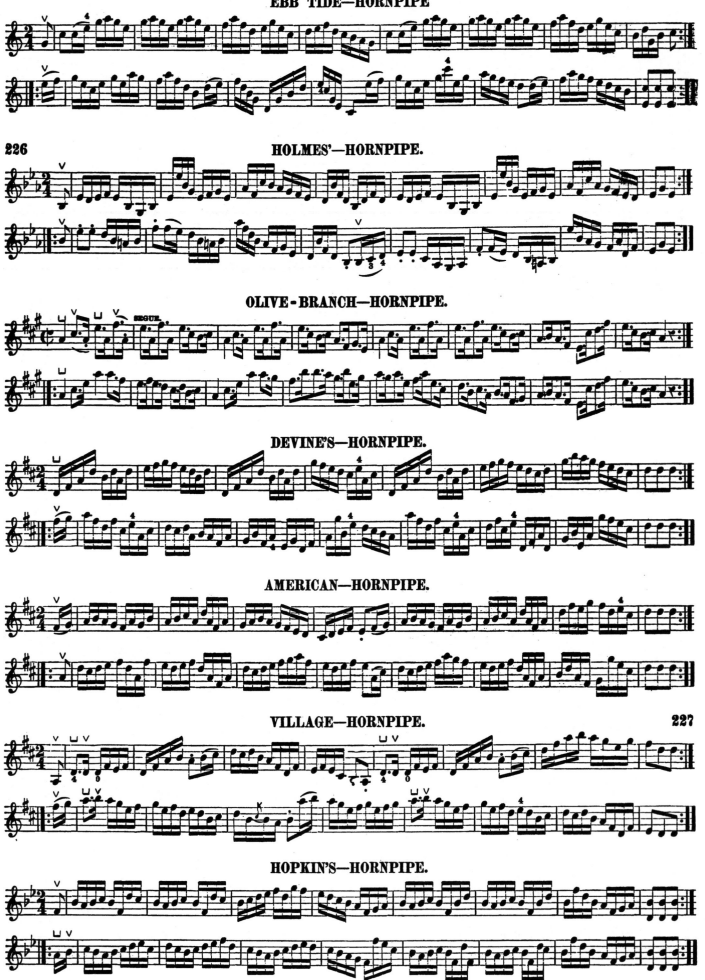

EBB TIDE—HORNPIPE

226

HOLMES'—HORNPIPE.

OLIVE - BRANCH—HORNPIPE.

DEVINE'S—HORNPIPE.

AMERICAN—HORNPIPE.

VILLAGE—HORNPIPE.

227

HOPKIN'S—HORNPIPE.

PRINCE REGENT'S—HORNPIPE.

HEWITSON'S—HORNPIPE.

228

CLEAR THE TRACK—HORNPIPE.
(Can be used as a Clog.)

CHRISTMAS—HORNPIPE.

CHRISTMAS HORNPIPE.—First lady balance to 1st and 2d gents, 3 hands round; First gent balance to 1st and 2d ladies, 3 hands round; First couple down the the centre, back, cast off; right and left 4.

CALEDONIAN LADDIE—HORNPIPE.

CONSTITUTION—HORNPIPE.

GOLDEN TRESSES—HORNPIPE. **229**
(Can be used as a Clog.)

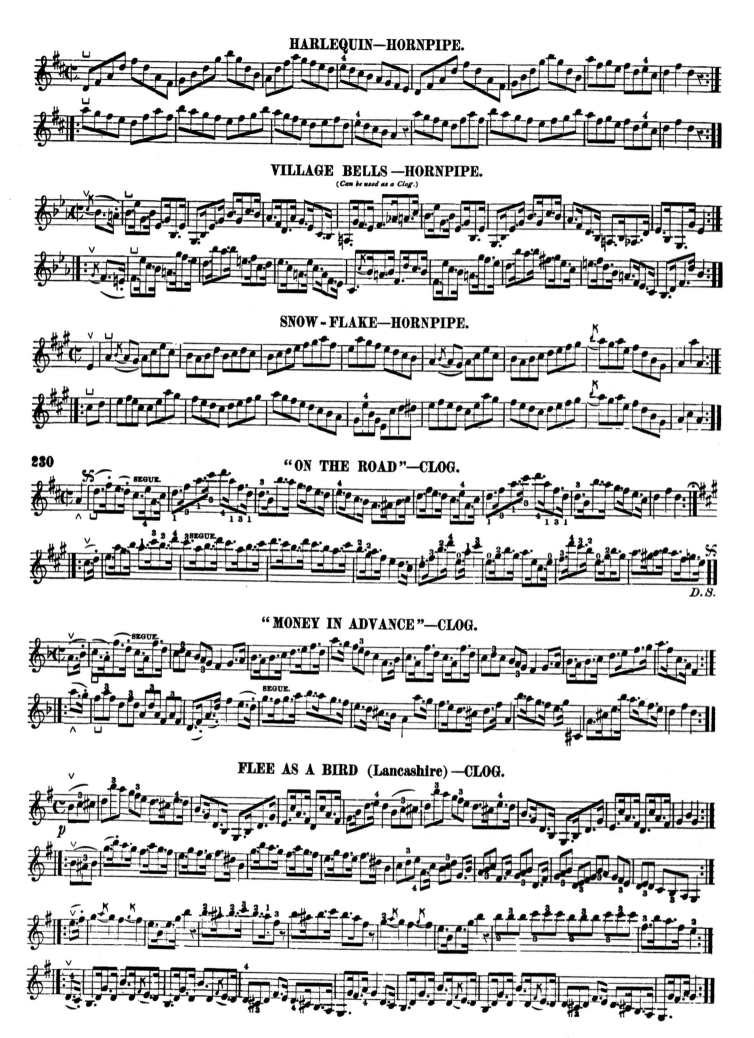

HARLEQUIN—HORNPIPE.

VILLAGE BELLS—HORNPIPE.
(Can be used as a Clog.)

SNOW-FLAKE—HORNPIPE.

230 "ON THE ROAD"—CLOG.

D.S.

"MONEY IN ADVANCE"—CLOG.

FLEE AS A BIRD (Lancashire)—CLOG.

154

STATUE—CLOG.

GREAT WESTERN (Lancashire)—CLOG.

NIGHTINGALE—CLOG.

THE MONARCH—CLOG.

EMPRESS—CLOG.

CITY LIFE—CLOG.

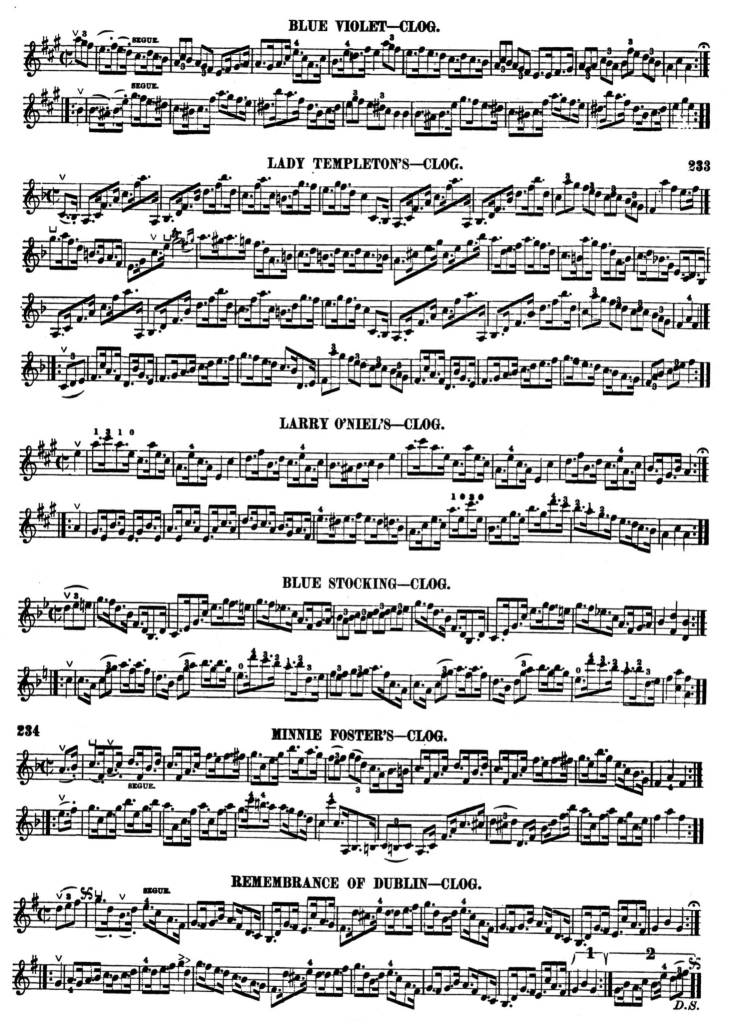

BLUE VIOLET—CLOG.

233

LADY TEMPLETON'S—CLOG.

LARRY O'NIEL'S—CLOG.

BLUE STOCKING—CLOG.

234

MINNIE FOSTER'S—CLOG.

REMEMBRANCE OF DUBLIN—CLOG.

MUNCIE'S FAVORITE (Lancashire)—CLOG.

NEW ORLEANS (Lancashire)—CLOG.

OLD IRONSIDES (Lancashire)—CLOG.

235

LOUISVILLE—CLOG.

FRANK LIVINGSTON.

TAMMANY RING—CLOG.

MINSTRELS' FANCY—CLOG.

236

NOVELTY (Lancashire)—CLOG.

F. A. MORRISON.

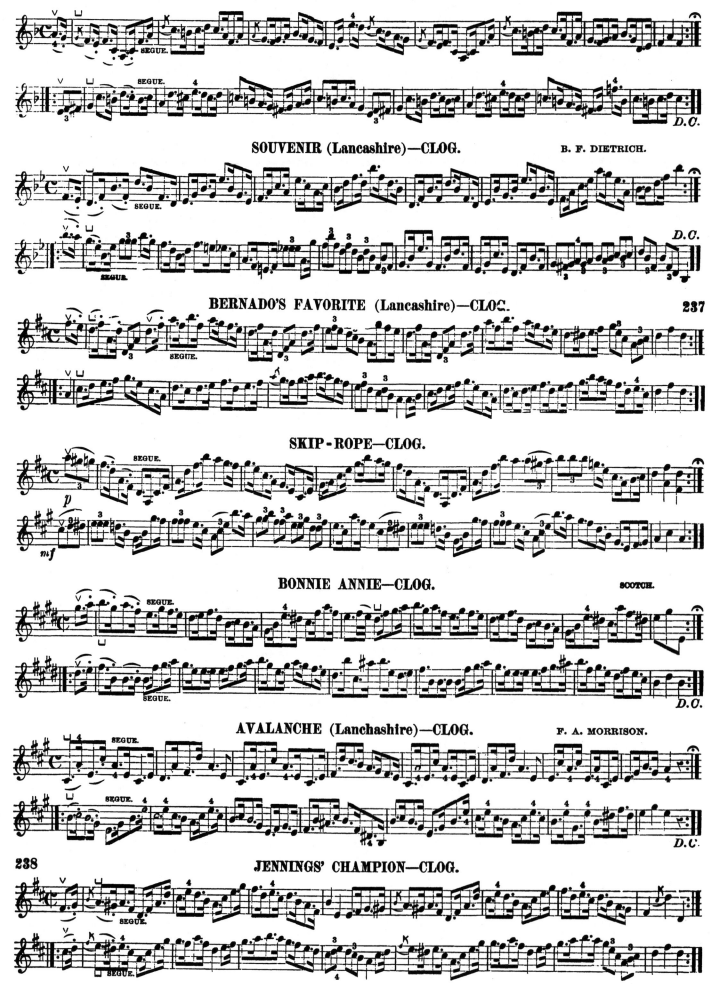

LOTUS CLUB (Lancashire)—CLOG.

SOUVENIR (Lancashire)—CLOG.

B. F. DIETRICH.

BERNADO'S FAVORITE (Lancashire)—CLOG.

237

SKIP-ROPE—CLOG.

BONNIE ANNIE—CLOG.

SCOTCH.

AVALANCHE (Lanchashire)—CLOG.

F. A. MORRISON.

238

JENNINGS' CHAMPION—CLOG.

EARLY MORN (Lanchashire)—CLOG.

EDWIN CHRISTIE.

DICK CARROL'S—CLOG.

JOHNNIE QUEEN'S—CLOG.

DICKIE ROGERS' PEDESTAL—CLOG.

239

GRAY'S OPERA HOUSE—CLOG.

BELLE OF THE STAGE (Lancashire)—CLOG.

EDWIN CHRISTIE.

FLY - BY - NIGHT (Lancashire)—CLOG.

CINCINNATI (Lancashire)—CLOG.

FRANK LIVINGSTON.

FISHERMANS' FROLIC (Lancashire)—CLOG.

CAMERON'S FAVORITE (Lancashire)—CLOG.

SCOTCH.

FAGAN AND FENTON'S—CLOG.

J. BRAHAM.

LEE'S DOUBLE—CLOG.

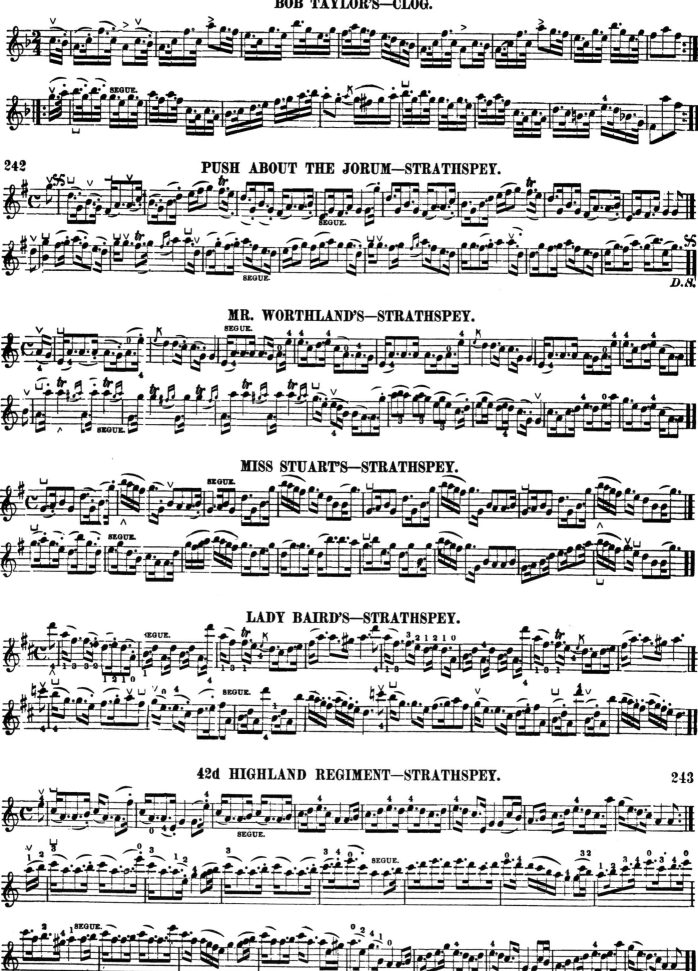

BOB TAYLOR'S—CLOG.

242   PUSH ABOUT THE JORUM—STRATHSPEY.

D.S.

MR. WORTHLAND'S—STRATHSPEY.

MISS STUART'S—STRATHSPEY.

LADY BAIRD'S—STRATHSPEY.

42d HIGHLAND REGIMENT—STRATHSPEY.   243

SANDY BUCHANAN'S—STRATHSPEY.

MY LADY'S GOON HAS GAIRS ON'T—STRATHSPEY.

STRATHEARN—STRATHSPEY.
Or "Among the Haughs of Cromdale."

LOCH-NA GAR—STRATHSPEY.

MRS. ADYE'S—STRATHSPEY.

LADY CHARLOTTE OF BRAID'S—STRATHSPEY.

ROY'S WIFE—STRATHSPEY.
As performed by NIEL GOW.

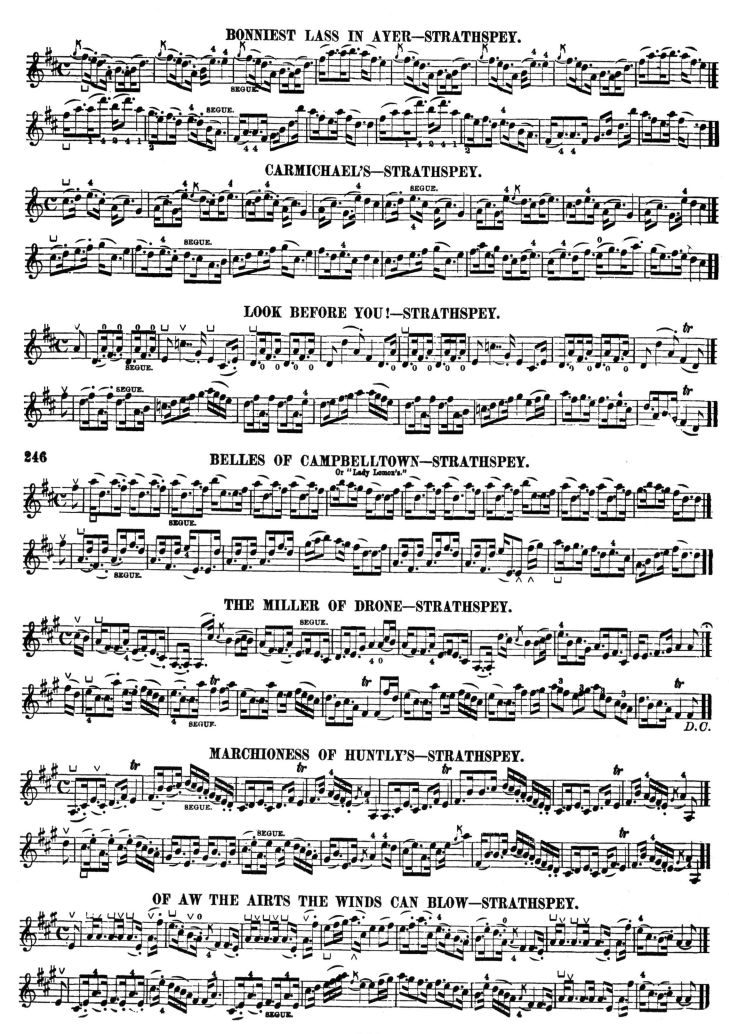

BONNIEST LASS IN AYER—STRATHSPEY.

CARMICHAEL'S—STRATHSPEY.

LOOK BEFORE YOU!—STRATHSPEY.

246 BELLES OF CAMPBELLTOWN—STRATHSPEY.
Or "Lady Lomon's."

THE MILLER OF DRONE—STRATHSPEY.

MARCHIONESS OF HUNTLY'S—STRATHSPEY.

OF AW THE AIRTS THE WINDS CAN BLOW—STRATHSPEY.

MISS DRUMMOND OF PERTH—STRATHSPEY.

SIR GEORGE CLARK'S—STRATHSPEY.

UP AND WAUR THEM A' WILLIE—STRATHSPEY.

CALEDONIAN HUNT—STRATHSPEY.

A' WILLIE, WE HAVE MISS'D YOU—STRATHSPEY.

LORD BYRON'S FAVORITE—STRATHSPEY.

WHAT THE DE'IL AILS YOU?—STRATHSPEY.

NEAL GOW'S WIFE—STRATHSPEY.

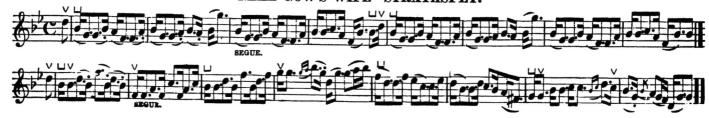

JARNOVICHES'—STRATHSPEY.

MY·LOVE IS LIKE THE RED, RED ROSE—STRATHSPEY.

THE NEW BRIG OF GLASGOW—STRATHSPEY.

GARTHLAND'S—STRATHSPEY.

LADY LOUDEN'S—STRATHSPEY.

ALISTAIR MACLALASTAIR—STRATHSPEY.

D.S.

DUCHESS OF ATHOL'S—STRATHSPEY.

THE LASS WITH THE YELLOW COATEE—STRATHSPEY.

LADY MARY RAMSAY'S—STRATHSPEY.   251

I'M O'ER YOUNG TO MARRY YET—STRATHSPEY.

MARQUIS OF HUNTLY'S—STRATHSPEY.

LORD ALEXANDER GORDON'S—STRATHSPEY.

252   MISS WARRENDER OF LOCHEND—STRATHSPEY.

THE BRAES OF BUSHBIE—STRATHSPEY.

LOCH EROCH SIDE—STRATHSPEY.

BANKS OF LOCK-NESS—STRATHSPEY.

MR. JAMES McNICOL'S—STRATHSPEY.

253

I'LL CLOOT MY JOHNNY'S GERY BREECKS—STRATHSPEY.

LADY ELGIN'S—STRATHSPEY.

THE BOATIE ROWS—STRATHSPEY.

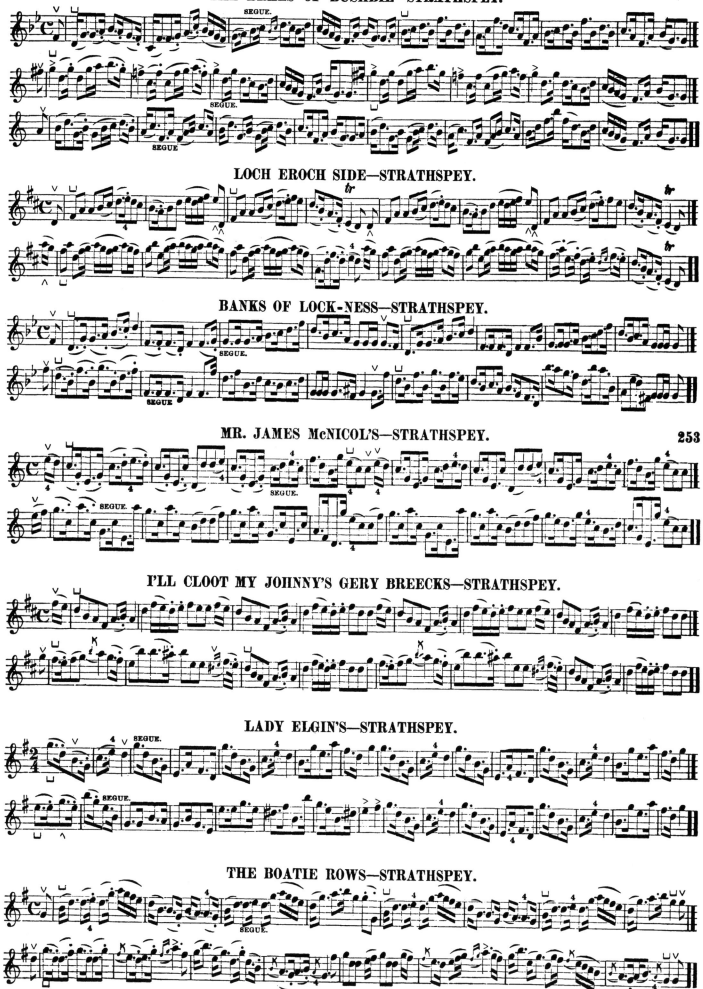

MONEY MUSK—STRATHSPEY.

MAID OF ISLA—STRATHSPEY.

DUNCAN DAVIDSON—STRATHSPEY.

LADY AMI STEWART'S—STRATHSPEY.

LORD JOHN CAMPBELL'S—STRATHSPEY.

BONNIE LASSIE—STRATHSPEY.

CALEDONIAN CLUB—STRATHSPEY.

EDWIN CHRISTIE.

OE'R THE MOOR, AMONG THE HEATHER—STRATHSPEY.

256 ECLIPSE—HIGHLAND FLING.

FOREST FLOWER—HIGHLAND FLING.

VILLAGE BELLS—HIGHLAND FLING.

MY BONNIE LADDIE—HIGHLAND FLING.

DOMINO—HIGHLAND FLING.

THE COTTAGE MAIDS'—FLING.   257

PRIDE OF THE STAGE—FLING.

169

TIBBIE INGLIS' FANCY—FLING.

FIRST FLIRTATION—FLING.

258 ROY'S WIFE—HIGHLAND FLING.

HERE AWA'—HIGHLAND FLING.

SCOTTISCH AMERICAN—HIGHLAND FLING.

MARQUIS OF HUNTLEY'S—HIGHLAND FLING.
(Can be used as a Strathspey.)

SINK HIM, DODDIE—HIGHLAND FLING. **259**
(Can be used as a Strathspey.)

170

BELLES OF EDINBORO'—HIGHLAND FLING.

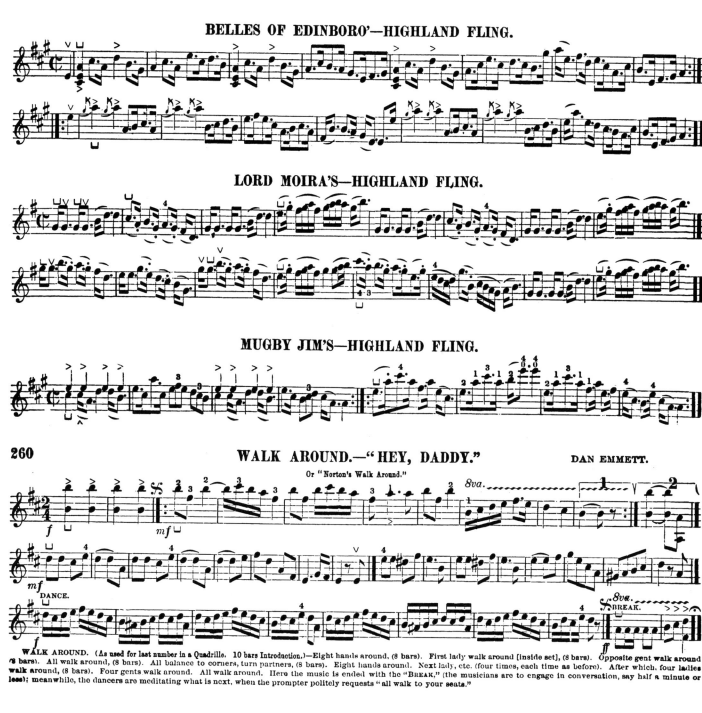

LORD MOIRA'S—HIGHLAND FLING.

MUGBY JIM'S—HIGHLAND FLING.

260

WALK AROUND.—"HEY, DADDY."

Or "Norton's Walk Around."

DAN EMMETT.

WALK AROUND. (As used for last number in a Quadrille. 10 bars Introduction.)—Eight hands around, (8 bars). First lady walk around [inside set], (8 bars). Opposite gent walk around (8 bars). All walk around, (8 bars). All balance to corners, turn partners, (8 bars). Eight hands around. Next lady, etc. (four times, each time as before). After which, four ladies walk around, (8 bars). Four gents walk around. All walk around. Here the music is ended with the "Break," (the musicians are to engage in conversation, say half a minute or less); meanwhile, the dancers are meditating what is next, when the prompter politely requests "all walk to your seats."

WALK AROUND.—DON'T GET WEARY.

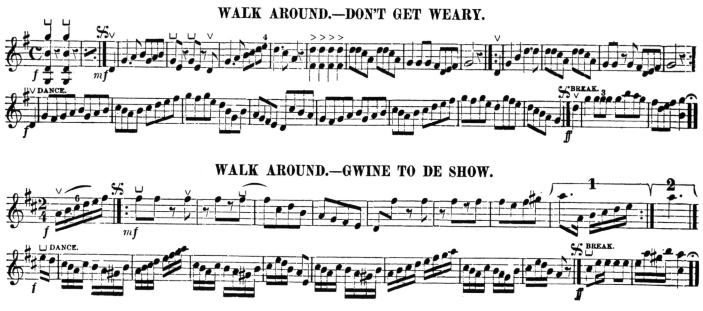

WALK AROUND.—GWINE TO DE SHOW.

WALK AROUND.—"CARVE DAT POSSUM."

WALK AROUND.—CARRY THE NEWS TO MARY.

WALK AROUND.—CHAW ROAST BEEF.

WALK AROUND.—"BRUDDER BONES."

ESSENCE OF CINNAMON SEED.

ESSENCE OF OLD VIRGINNY.

ESSENCE OF SUGAR CANE.

ESSENCE OF OLD KENTUCKY.

NEW BOSTON SICILLIAN CIRCLE.

SICILLIAN CIRCLE.—Right and left. Cross four hands half round, back with left hands. Ladies chain. All forward and back, forward, pass by to next couples. [Repeat.]

SWEET ELLEN, (or Figure Eight.)

FIGURE EIGHT.—First couple cross over, [inside] below second couple, down centre, return [outside] to head. Again cross over [inside] down centre, back [outside] to places. First couple down centre, back, cast off. Right and left.

ROY'S WIFE OF ALDIVALLOCH.

ROY'S WIFE.—First couple join right hands and balance, [4 bars], down the centre [4 bars], balance at the foot [4 bars], back to places [4 bars], cross 4 hands with second couple, back with left hands [8 bars]. Right and left with same couple, [8 bars].

THE "GOOD GIRL."

GOOD GIRL.—First lady turn second gent., first gent. turn second lady. Four hands half round, and back to places. Two couples down centre, back, first couple cast off. Right and left 4.

264

NEUMEDIA.

POP GOES THE WEASEL.

"POP GOES THE WEASEL."

POP GOES THE WEASEL.—First couple down the outside, back. Down the centre, back. Three hands half round with second lady; first couple raise hands, second lady pops under to place. First couple three hands half round with second gent; first couple raise hands, second gent pops under to place.

SOLDIERS' JOY.

SOLDIERS' JOY, [Form a circle, two couples facing].—Forward and back four, turn the opposite. Balance and turn partners. Ladies chain. Forward and back, forward, pass by to next couple.

THE TEMPEST.

TEMPEST. [Form in two lines, of couples facing]. First two couples down the centre, abreast, turn half round [ladies remaining at the right of partners], and back. Balance to the sides, [each couple], four hands round. Right and left.

PETRONELLA.

SCOTCH. 265

PETRONELLA.—(Form as for Contra Dance.) First couple to the right, balance opposite each other in centre of set, [4 bars]. Again to the right, and balance on sides of set, [4 bars]. Again to the right, and balance in centre of set, [4 bars]. Again to the right, and balance to places [4 bars]. Down the centre and back, [8 bars]. Cast off, right and left 4, [8 bars].

CHORUS—JIG.

CHORUS JIG.—First couple down the outside, back. Down the centre, back. Turn contra corners. Balance, turn partners to places.

THE GIRL I LEFT BEHIND ME.

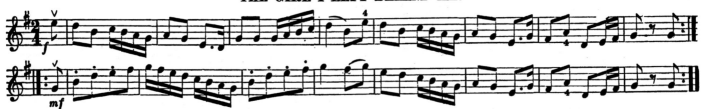

FORTY STUDIES FOR THE VIOLIN.

Designed for those not having the advantage of a Teacher.

⌣ **Denotes Down Bow.**   ⋁ **Denotes Up Bow.**   **Segue:—Indicates go on in same manner.**

The following Ten Studies should be played slowly, using whole bow for each note ; having practised faithfully, in this manner, they should be played faster, using a third of the bow in the middle, care being taken to play the notes evenly, with full tone and good intonation.

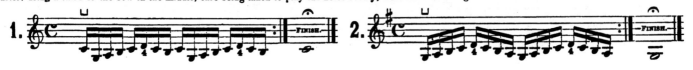

No. 11. Take first two notes with short down and up bow at the heel; for slurred notes, use whole bow, which, when repeated will bring the two dotted (or staccato) notes with an up and down bow at the point, and so on, changing at each repeat.

No. 12. Take first note with down bow to the point, upper two thirds of the bow for slurred notes, which will in repeating bring the first staccato note with an up bow, changing at each repeat.

No. 13. Play slowly at first, with whole bow, then faster in the middle of the bow.

No. 14. Take first note with a *darting* down bow, (upper two thirds.)

Nos. 15 & 16. The first eighth note with whole down bow; the following sixteenths with short bow at point; the next eighth with whole up bow; the following sixteenths with short bow at the heel.

Nos. 17 & 18. In the middle of the bow, with forearm.

No. 19. Must be played with a whole bow, evenly.

No. 20. Use whole bow at first slowly, then faster, in the middle.

No. 21. Must be played with a whole bow, evenly.

No. 22. Must be played in the middle of the bow, well marked.

No. 23. Must be played in the middle of the bow, well marked.

No. 24. Execute in the middle of the bow, as marked.

No. 25. The first two slurred notes are taken with a down bow, (upper half), from middle to point; the two dotted notes with an up and down bow, (upper third), and so on the slurred notes with down and up bow alternately

No. 26. The two dotted notes are taken with a down and up bow, (upper half), the two slurred notes with down bow, which is the reverse of the preceding study.

No. 27. Take the four slurred notes with a down bow, from the middle to the point; the four dotted notes at the point of the bow; the next four slurred notes with an up bow to the middle, and so on alternately.

No. 28. Take first four notes with four short bowings, in the middle of the bow, and is then played like the preceding number.

29.

No. 29. Take first two notes with a down bow; next two with an up bow, (in the middle of bow): use equal amount of bow, both down and up, thereby keeping the bow in same position. Count four in a measure, slowly. This style of bowing is used in playing Clogs, Strathspeys, etc.

30.

No. 30. Execute slowly, in the same manner as the preceding study.

31.

No. 31. Execute in the middle of the bow, observing the same principles of bowing as in the two preceding studies.

32.

No. 32. Use middle of bow, (count three in a measure) accenting first note in each measure. Must be played very equal and Staccato.

1. Executed in the middle third of the bow, very slowly at first, with an equality of tone and correct intonation.

2. Use whole down bow for the three slurred notes, and a short up and down bow at the point for the two dotted or staccato notes; the three following slurred notes with a whole up bow, which brings the bow into its first position, and so on.

3. Use whole down bow for the two slurred notes, and the two staccato notes, with an up and down bow at the point; the two following slurred notes with a whole up bow, and the two staccato notes with a down and up bow at the heel alternately.

4. Use a short down and up bow at the heel for first two notes; a whole down bow for the two following slurred notes; a short up and down bow at the point for the two staccato notes; a whole up bow for the two following slurred notes.

5. Take the first note with a short down bow, (middle) and the following thirty-second note with an up bow, under the same length of bow as for the dotted sixteenth note, thereby keeping the bow in same position throughout.

6. Begin with an up bow—which will be the preceding study reversed.—The bowing to the following study is mostly used.

7. Take first two notes with down bow, (upper half) use nearly all of the upper half of the bow for the dotted sixteenth note, the remainder for the thirty-second note; the two following notes with an up bow, same as two preceding notes, and so on, (i. e.) two down and two up.

8. Use the upper fourth part of the bow, (or the point) with a firm arm stroke, using only the fore arm, the back arm remaining as motionless as possible.

The following Study is to be executed throughout, as indicated by the Eight Models above.

ALLEGRO MODERATO.